Adam:
The Universally-Evolving, Human Soul, Male & Female

Also by Hameed El Amin:

"The Good Sense that G'd Gave." New Shoes Educational Publishers. Normal Alabama, 1996.
"Education for Faith-Based Intelligence and Commuity Life." New Shoes Educational Publishers. Normal Alabama, 1998.
"A History of Muslim African-Americans." Associate-Editor, WDM Publications, 2007.

Adam:
The Universally-Evolving, Human Soul, Male & Female

> Scriptural Reasoning & Wholistic Principled-Logic for the Social & Material Sciences, Evolving Institutions for Post-Modern Civilization.
>
> Language & Logic for Informing the Study & Application of the Spiritual Sciences to the Social & Material Sciences.

Writer/Scribe/Author
Hameed El Amin, B.A. Morehouse College
MS, PhD, The University of Massachusetts, Amherst

Adam: The Universally-Evolving, Human Soul, Male & Female

Copyright © 2024 by Hameed El Amin, PhD

All Rights Reserved. Printed in the United States of America. No part of this book may be reproduced or utilized in any manner electronic, manual or otherwise, including photocopying or recording of any information via any storage system without express permission of the writer/scribe/author.

The author may be reached at hameedel@msn.com

Editing, Cover & Typesetting by Book Power Publishing

Published by New Shoes Educational Publishers

ISBN Paperback: 978-1-945873-80-5
ISBN Hardcover: 978-1-945873-81-2
ISBN Ebook: 978-1-945873-79-9

New Shoes Educational Publishers

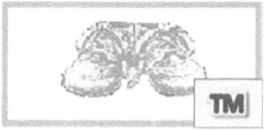

As-Saliheen

This work is dedicated to As-Saliheen,
the sincere and right minded of every nation, tribe and
people among all of Mankind.

Author's Note

"Adam: The Universally-Evolving Human Soul, Male & Female" is the first book in a series on the language, logic and principles influencing Post-Modern, cultural logic, socially-constructed reality, and institutional establishment. The focus of this series is a detailed analysis of exaggerated schemes that falsify language, logic, science, philosophy, and social and cultural constructions.

Universal respect for the common soul as a plural body and a unity of spirit, thinking, reason and the principled logic of science, are necessary for evolving peace on earth for every human soul in the Post-Modern World.

Understanding Mankind as a plural body created from one soul is a foundational principle that moderates the predatory competition, the "religious," ideological, philosophical, cultural, racial and ethnic extremes. Extremes of Man's social and cultural constructs that promote domination of the universal soul created, belonging to and guided by Allah, G'd and Lord of All the Systems of Knowledge.

The logic and language of this series evolves and is informed by Qur'anic logic, the commentary of "America's Imam" Imam Warith Deen Mohammed (raa), and the work of many of his students.

HAE 12/16/2023

Contents

Author's Note	vi
Preface	xiii
Introduction	xx

Part One
"50,000 Years!" "The End of that Road, the Exact Sciences." 1

Chapter One 2
- "FORCES OF NATURE ARE BRINGING IN THE WORLD G'D WANTS." IWDM 2
- Adam, the Evolving Human Soul From Spiritual Origins to Social & Material Sciences For Building Houses With the Universals of Civilized Life, Abraham (as) 3
- An Al Qur'an as Source, Ascension-Based, Creation-Inspired Framework for Re-rooting & Unifying Knowledge, Education & the Sciences 3
- Materialism, Deconstruction & Dissembling of the Sciences 4
- The Evolution of Adam (as) the Archetypal Mind & Soul: A Post-Modern Critique of Bio-Genic Evolution 5
- "Natural Evolution Blocked by Man's Constructions" 5
- Psyché as Mind & Soul 8
- "Human Identity" Imam Warith Deen Mohammed (raa) 10
- "Man is Spiritual and Expresses Himself Materially" IWDM 10
- "Potential, Male and Female." IWDM 11
- "You Have a Male Side and a Female Side." IWDM 11

Chapter Two 12
- "Man Means Mind, and Words Make People." — IWDM 13
- The Unseen (Bil Gaib) 16
- A Post-Modern View of Evolution From the Archetypal Soul to Genes & the Genesis of Man as Mind 16
- The Gen (Jinn), Genius & Adam Redefining the Fulfillment of Human Potential 17
- Meta-Physics, Genes, Genesis & the Epigenesis of Genius 19

Chapter Three 23
- Brain Science 23
- The Evolution of the Psyche´ as Mind, Soul & Self (*Nafs*): A Post-Modern View for "The Day of Religion" (*Yawm ud Deen*) 25

Part Two
Scriptural Reasoning, Axiomatic Principles & Metaphysical Logic As Support For The Social & Material & Objective Sciences 26

Chapter Four 28
- "We Don't Know What We Don't Know!" 28
- Fajr & Fujur The Dawn of Reason 30
- Innate, Inherent or Inborn Sensibilities & Faculties Mechanistic Brain Science as Deconstruction of The Soul 33
- The Brain Is Hardware, the Heart Is the Sensitive Life 37

Chapter Five 39
- The Soul+ Archetypal Nature + Nurture & Epigenetic Influences 39
- Socially Constructed Language Environments 41
- Racism & Sexism as Socially-Constructed Macro-Aggressions, in the Social, Material & Objective Sciences 43
- The Recycled Boogey Men of Color: "Reverse Racism," "Critical Race Theory," & "DEI" 45
- Freud & Psychosexual Theory, A Mind Full of Sex & Aggression 46
- Experience, Subjective & Objective Awareness 47

Chapter Six 49
- The Deconstruction & Devolution of Adam as the First Mind 50
- "Truth Stands Out Clear from Error." 51

Part Three
"Ulul Al Bab" Those Who Open The Doors To The Sciences 54

Chapter Seven 55
- The Good News, Sura 78, An-Naba, Verse #19 55
- "Pursue G'd's Creation for its Knowledge & its Sciences." Imam Warith Deen Mohammed (raa) 55
- The Application of Al Qur'an & Scriptural Reasoning as Renewed Sources of Knowledge 57

- "Lord of All the Systems of Knowledge" 58
- "Read! in the Name of Thy Lord and Cherisher…" 59
- Man as Mind Stands Upon the Two Legs of Common Sense & Rational Sense 60
- One Soul, Two Feet, & Two Legs 61
- "Dry" Logic The Modern-Day Perspectives of Academics 63
- Systematizing & Evolving Language Environments 65
- Sharing Models & Strategies of Best Practice 65
- Redefining Academics: A Potential in Every Human Soul 66

Chapter Eight 68
- Prayer of the Muslims for Jews and Christians 68
- "Who are the followers of Abraham?" 68
- Keeping Knowledge Whole, the Covenant of Abraham (as)" IWDM 68
- The Ascension of the Soul "Worlds Revolving Around a Core…" IWDM 69
- "Man, Who Has to Be Responsible For Society." 70
- "Worlds Revolving Around a Core," "Seven in Earth & Seven in Light" IWDM 70
- Strategic Analysis with the Ascension of the Soul Construct: Aligning Two Worlds of Reality: The Social World & The Natural World 72
- Reclaiming Academics - Ascension Level 5 - Idris: A Potential in Every Human Soul 72
- Archetypes, Architects, Social Engineers & Culture: Archetypal Patterns of the Human Soul 74
- Socially-Constructed Barriers of Cryptic Language & Logic 75
- "Language Construction is Most Important." IWDM 77
- Every Bird Needs Both Wings 80
- Living Our Best Life Is Living Our Shared Life 81
- Dividing the Mates 83

Chapter Nine 86
- Chattel Slavery an Experiment in Crucifying Human Soul 90
- Cryptic, or Hidden, Logic & Language Speaks Over the Head of Academic, "Dry" Logic 91
- Artificial Language Uproots the Spirit & Word of Creation From the Logic of Culture 92
- "Connect Knowledge."- Imam Warith Deen Mohammed 92
- Scriptural Reasoning, Academics, Language & Logic for Evolving the Spirit & Intellect & Building Every House 95

- Conventional Meanings of Language Are Man-Made & Therefore Can Become Artificial.. 96
- Imam Warith Deen Mohammed (raa) on Word Study..................... 96
- Meeting Places # One High Places 98
- In Language Construction, the Picture is the Word! 101
- A Thousand Words for An Apple?.. 102

Chapter Ten 104
- The Separation of Modern Philosophy & the Rational Sciences, From the Dogma of Religion 104
- Social Engineering.. 105
- Revelation (Wahy) from Scripture & (Wahy) From the Book of Creation 106
- The Ka'bah, the Universal House & Universal Language Environment 107

Part Four
Wholistic Principled Logic as Support for The Academic or Rational Sciences 109

Chapter Eleven 110
- Whole, Holy, Wholly & Wholistic Language & Logic 110
- "The Mountains' Means 'Wise, Informed, Above Small Visions…'" IWDM... 113
- Epistemology/Etymology "Study from the Root of Knowledge." IWDM... 114
- Study the Nature of All Forms, Language & Logic 115
- Rote Memory, Training & Repetition, Create Spirit Without Meaning & Understanding.. 116
- Creation-Inspired Constructions of Language Environments............. 118
- "Education in Creation" Nuurah Amatullah Muhammed, MAT, (raa) 119
- Satan Colors the Spirit & Mind with Skin, Crawling in the Dust of Surface Language.. 120
- Race is Not a Card!... 122

Chapter Twelve 123
- The Tree as a Sign for Evolving the Goodly Spirit & Intelligent Life ... 123
- Artificial Language Environments & Crucify the Body as Symbolic Knowledge 124
- "The Media Makes Leaders." IWDM 125

- No Fool No Fun! 126
- "Gog" (Head) & "Magog" (No Head) IWDM 129
- The Mentally & Spiritually Dead 132
- Division in the Social & Material Sciences Creates Division in the Soul & Psyché 135
- The Spirit & Word Evolve from the Soul. 137
- Corrupt Means to Break the Heart 138
- Satan Lies in Wait in Language Environments 140
- The Cross: "A Sign of the Original State that (G'd) Allah Made the Soul to Be In." IWDM 141
- Language Environments Provide the Breath of Life 142
- Keep Your Feet on the Ground & Your Head to the Sky! 143
- G'd's Promise to Abraham in Genesis 144
- Goodness Rising 146

Part Five
Remaking The World of Academics with Universal Concepts & Scriptural Reasoning.   148

Chapter Thirteen   149
- "Four Days Measure Supplied all Things" – IWDM 149
- "The Sciences" IWDM 150
- Cultural Insanity: The Socially-Constructed, Recycled Influences of Culture Wars 151
- Cultural Insanity, Socially-Constructed Influences, & Clinical Symptoms 151
- Racism and Sexism As Classic Cases of Macro-Aggression ... 152
- Slaves as Three fifths of a Man, A Socially Constructed Macro-Aggression! 153
- "A Sacred Rule" Of Socially Constructed Hierarchies 154
- Macro-Aggressions & Micro-Aggressions, Cultural Insanity & Communal Trauma in Language Environments 154
- Recycling of Macro-Aggressions & Micro-Aggressions 157
- Archetypal Culture Wars 162
- It's Wake-up Time! 164

Chapter Fourteen   165
- Socially-Constructed Language Barriers To Scriptural Reasoning, Common Sense, & the Universals of Education 166
- Al Qur'an, Creation, Rational Sciences & Man's Constructions 167

- "The Need for Volumes on Science & Scientific Theory" IWDM 168
- From "Bean Soup Science" to Support of Academics with Scriptural Reasoning 169
- "We Should Come Together, Share What We Have, Then Go Home & Do Our Work." IWDM 170
- Shura Baynahum as Sharing of Ideas 171
- A Method of Research from America's Imam "Test What We are Going to Use." IWDM.. 172
- Urges as Movements in the Soul "Four Rivers, Four Birds & Four Mountains in Human Nature as Efforts to Educate & Develop Culture." IWDM 172
- "Aligning the Natural World & the Social World." 174
- A Model for Evolving Freedom, Free Thinking, Collaborative Effort, Shared Vision, Local Responsibility & Leadership "African-American Leadership." IWDM... 175

Epilogue & Past as Prologue 177
- Evolving a Series of Studies 177
- Natural Urges in Human Life, Give Rise to Social Science, the Logic & Ethics of Institutions, Culture & Civilized Life! 178
- We Live by Faith, We Progress by Knowledge & Reason. 180
- A Personal Reflection from a Letter to a Childhood Friend................ 180
- Mr. Jefferson of Monticello 185

About the Author 187
Writer/Scribe 188
Abbreviations 189
Collaboration: 189
Works Cited & References 190
References.. 193
Citations of Sura & Ayat of Al Qur'an.. 196
About the Cover 199

Preface

Adam: The Universally-Evolving, Human Soul, Male & Female

Language & Logic for Informing the Study & Application of the Spiritual Sciences to the Social & Material Sciences

Chapter (90) Sūrat l-Balad (The City)

> 8."Have We not made for him a pair of eyes? 9. And a tongue and a pair of lips? 10. "And showed him the two highways? 11. "But he hath made no haste on the path that is steep." Al Qur'an, Yusuf Ali, S. 90, A. 8-11.

Freeing the Slave of Socially-Constructed Exaggerations & Rational Lies in Culture & Objective Sciences

Chapter (90) Sūrat l-Balad (The City)

> "And what will explain to thee the path that is steep?"
> "[It is] to free a slave." Al Qur'an, Yusuf Ali, S. 90, A. 12-13.

"Do Not Forget Your Share of the Material World." Imam Warith Deen Mohammed(raa)

Chapter (28) Sūrat l-Qasas (The Stories)

> "But seek, with the (wealth) which Allah has bestowed on thee, the Home of the Hereafter, nor forget thy portion in this world: but do thou good, as Allah has been good to thee, and seek not (occasions for) mischief in the land: for Allah loves not those who do mischief." Al Qur'an, Yusuf Ali, S. 28, A. 77.

"The Qur'an Came to Reconcile the Spiritual Concepts with the Material Concepts." — Imam Warith Deen Mohammed

> "So, we know that the Qur'an came for that purpose, to reconcile the spiritual concepts with the material concepts, to bring back the unity of the sciences, where the spiritual concepts are not at odds with material needs and material life. We cannot live fighting material life and material kinds of interests and concerns. We have to be in accord with that, we have to appreciate those concerns, because those are necessities of our being. " — Imam Mohammed, Warith Deen (raa). "Symbolic Language," 1984, Harlem, N.Y. Lecture.

"Adam: The Universally-Evolving, Human Soul, Male and Female" is the first title in a series of monographs that inform the evolution and establishment of a renewed approach to universal values for cultural life and civilized progress. This series of monographs discusses the implications of understanding Adam (as) as the universal, human soul. This renewed approach to the human soul seeks to remedy Modern-Day insufficiencies in culture, social constructions, and civilized progress in "the Day of Religion" (Yawm ud Deen).

Culture encompasses all of Man's material creations, ideas, influences and social constructions. This requires that we ask ourselves, "Is the cultural and social environment into which we are born the most influential of all the socially constructed circumstances that define us as individuals?"

The big picture for evolving conscious life is culture, and the language and logic of culture are the construction of men, by G'd's permission. Culture and social constructions should respect the common soul, the logic of nature, the faculties of thinking, the universals of human nature and the guidance of revelation.

The logic of this renewed model of social construction is:

1. G'd gives guidance to the spirit and reason of man through revelation and the lives of the Prophets (as), especially the life example (Uswah) of the model man, the Prophet Muhammed (saw).
2. Abraham (as) is the Father of Reason and Faith and builder of the Ka'bah, which represents the universal spiritual and rational underpinnings of society. The Prophet Muhammad (saw) is the fulfillment of the work of Abraham and all the Prophets (as). Man uses reason to construct ideas and bring social life into agreement with revelation, the spirit and thinking of the original Soul (Adam) and the principles of the natural world.

The logic for evolving institutions, is used to constructs language environments based on universals of culture that support:

1. Education
2. Culture (especially entertainment and ideas)
3. Business, and
4. Government.

Every human soul depends upon, and is influenced by, each of these institutions from birth. Institutions enable us to become socially responsible individuals through free thinking, the shared benefits of productive effort and other standards of earned merit for advancement in civilized life.

"Throw Out All of Their Books."
Imam Warith Deen Mohammed (raa)

"Make an intelligent analysis of the situation of inferiority and then come up with right recommendations. The educators in this community can do this. Don't go out there and look for a psychology book or social behavior book in the library. You lock

yourself up – throw out all of their books. Only use the dictionary. Only use the book that will give you terminology.

But don't use any book that suggests a philosophy or suggests a principle, or suggests a way of behaving or psychology... Just reject it all and take your Qur'an and take what we have in this community. And lock the door. Say there is a strong temptation to 'pick up a white man' and then lean on him. To avoid that, we are going to keep all of their literature out while we design the course that we should take." — Imam Mohammed, Warith Deen (raa). "Educational Concerns." Historic Sedalia Address, 9 April 1982. Lecture.

"The Haqq & Ayat of Creation & Revelation"
Imam Dr. Bashir Ali

Chapter (41) Sūrat Fussilat

"Soon will We show them our Signs in the (furthest) regions (of the earth), and in their own souls, until it becomes manifest to them that this is the Truth. Is it not enough that thy Lord doth witness all things?" Al Qur'an, Yusuf Ali , S. 41, A. 53.

There are more than 21 million books in the Library of Congress. As pointed out by Imam Dr. Bashir Ali, for Muslims, the sciences of creation (Wahy) can be brought into agreement with the logic of Al Qur'an. Al Qur'an is the final book of revelation (Wahy), revealed by the Lord of All the Systems of Knowledge. Haqq ul Yaqin is "the truth of assured certainty" that belongs to Allah alone as Lord of All the Systems of Knowledge. Al Qur'an is the source of truth which points to every sign (Ayah) in creation. Al Qur'an clarifies every book of science, every socially constructed idea , cultural logic and every language construct for building civilized life.

Al Qur'an is the "truth of assured certainty" (Haqqul Yaqin), its divine language, logic and grammar revealed to the last Prophet

Muhammad of Arabia (saw). We may critique all of the language constructions of Modern-Day Science, academic language and logic and their application to social constructions with Al Qur'an.

Every book of creation-inspired knowledge can be critiqued by studying the origin of words (etymology) and the epistemological origins of the knowledge that established civilization. Although English is composed of root meanings from other languages including dead languages like Latin, English is the primary language of Modern-Day Sciences around the world.

Imam Mohammed (raa) noted in a curriculum meeting in 2001, "We want to teach the subjects required for the level of education. That's what we want to teach, but we want to influence that teaching with Qur'an!" The subjects are the Social Sciences and the Creation-Inspired Sciences that establish Man in the productive life of material creation and civilized progress. These subjects evolve language environments for establishing the Rational Sciences, Man's cultural logic and the spiritual and rational foundations for constructing institutions. As pointed out by Imam Dr. Bashir Ali, the Haqq and Ayat of Creation-Inspired Sciences and the root meanings of the language and logic of every science can be informed by Al Qur'an — the G'd-given Book that informs all the systems of knowledge.

A Shura-Based, Collaborative Model for Sharing Ideas & Model Lessons

"We should come together, share what we have, then go home and do our work." — Imam Mohammed, Warith Deen (raa). August 3, 2008, Homewood, IL. Lecture.

The purpose of our collaborative, Shura-based model of sharing ideas is to establish the work of the Sister Clara Muhammad Memorial

Education Foundation Clearing House and to promote shared vision, free thinking, and individual responsibility toward the establishment of an institution "that will outlive us all" (Imam Mohammed (raa).

Collaborators from the Education Workgroup of the Sister Clara Mohammed Memorial Education Foundation and Education Consortium contributed to the clarity of this work.

> **WORD STUDY**
>
> of Study & Student
>
> "To *study* is to strive towards, devote oneself to, or cultivate."
>
> Harper, & Liu, Etymonline.com
>
> Interpretation
>
> *Student* = one who strives towards
>
> cultivating spirit and thinking.

Imam Warith Deen Mohammed (raa) on Word Study

"What I am giving you is more important than what Moses brought down from the mountain." — Imam Mohammed, Warith Deen (raa). "Saviors Day Lecture." 2007, Chicago, IL. Lecture.

How will we begin to update all the books of the academic, "dry" logic and language perspectives of Modern-Day Rational Sciences, culture, knowledge, and systems of education of the last 500 years with Scriptural Reasoning? We must begin with the language and logic of Al Qur'an to study the origin of every word in the Social and Material Sciences as logic for informing reason through the study of Allah's creation. This must be done in light of the language and logical connections with the certainty of knowing the Haqqul Yaqin of revelation. We pray that Allah (swt) — Al Aziz, Al Hakim — continues to bless our efforts of working and evolving together as one human soul.

Throughout this monograph, you will see boxes labeled WORD STUDY. These are call-out boxes in which we will dive deeply into the study of words in the English language, using references to interpret refined meanings of specific terms in the context of our evolving paradigm.

The "Dead Letter" of Uprooted, Language, Logic & Artificial Culture

> "We want an institution that will outlive you and you and you and me."— Imam Warith Deen Mohammed (raa). May 5, 2008, Eat Rice Lunch, Homewood, IL. Conversation.

The understanding and description of individual clinical symptoms, diagnostic criteria, and the symptom picture of personal or individual insanity are similarly reflected in Cultural Insanity. This "better from him" rather than "better than him," as translated and explained by Imam Qasim Ahmed (raa), is a profound Qur'anic insight into the beginning of the problem as a rebellious potential of every human soul. A spirit and mentality that seek to dominate and control every influence on civilized life through self-serving power, scientifically-exaggerated philosophical or socially-constructed ideological influences in social life and culture. We call that mindset Shaitan, the oldest-but-never-grown-up, teen rebel in the Garden, and we seek refuge from Shaitan in our own selves!

Introduction

Chapter (31) Sūrat Luq'mān

"And if all the trees on earth were pens and the ocean (was ink) with seven oceans more to add to its (supply) yet would not the words of Allah be exhausted (in the writing): for Allah is Exalted in Power, full of Wisdom." Al Qur'an, Yusuf Ali, S. 31, A. 27.

This monograph, "Adam, the Universally Evolving, Human Soul, Male & Female," is the first of a series addressing a broad scope of Social Science topics and their logical connections to individual life with social systems. These topics will address the archetypal origins of civilized life and their intimate connection to emerging principles, social constructions, and principled logic for the evolution of institutions in the "Day of Religion."

"The Slave Girl Shall Give Birth to Her Master." Hadith of Prophet Muhammad (saw)

Coloring the Mind with Skin is Oppression for Every Human Soul.

We may propose that it is us, African-Americans, who have advanced the freedom, justice, and equality of all for our nation, alongside others who have struggled toward universal freedom for the human soul since the founding fathers of these United States established the principles of freedom, justice, and equality for all. Among the citizens and present-day public servants of our country, who has not seen the long and difficult struggle and still finds difficulty supporting the Post-Modern evolution toward universal equality for every human soul?

It Was Not a Long Time

As students of the Social Sciences, we have derived numerous lessons from socially-constructed , influences and the misuse of power. These hard-earned lessons are imbued with an epigenetic urge clocked into my genes from my mother's grandmother, Martha Gresham, born a slave in 1860. An American slave in whose lap I sat and whose hard-earned wrinkles I touched while she warmed her bones in the afternoon sun of the Spring of 1947.

It absolutely was not a long time ago — as our "woke" and anti-woke, self-interested culture warriors wish it to be! It was not a long time ago that African-American slaves lost their personal, social, cultural, and human identities and the right as human beings to own their skin. Yet, they kept the spirit of faith that preserved the souls of many by G'd's Mercy. Until every human soul is redeemed, this "original sin" will be recycled in social life and culture.

Peoples of all identities are created archetypally from one human soul, but are falsely identified by skin, ethnic identity, lifestyle choice, gender, social status, ethnicity, nationality, and political persuasion — rather than as Man as spirit and thinking.

Humanity has endured a prolonged struggle for centuries due to the "original sin" of continually-recycled, falsified, devalued human identities. Having been stripped of human identity by chattel slavery, African Americans endured four centuries of working, praying, repenting, forgiving, and suffering to improve the shared human identity. A struggle that has benefitted every human soul in reclaiming the social sentiments of shared humanity from the influences of the common foe Satan, the enemy that begins within the soul and the universal enemy of all Mankind.

Respect for the spirit, thinking, language, logic, ethics, and universals of reason — originating in and supported by faith — are part of the founding principles and G'd-given inheritance for our struggle to free the human soul by the Will of G'd.

G'd has continually blessed America with generations who teach, struggle, and remind us to keep our faith and common sense and to plant our feet firmly on the ground in service to that sacred obligation.

The archetypal desire is for a radical evolution of freedom as the destiny for which every human soul, created equal, seeks freedom and justice for all. And may G'd grant Mercy to all the righteous people (As-Saliheen) of every nation, tribe, and people, here and in the gardens of paradise, as He Wills! The shared effort of this work aims to support the evolution of the Plural Body, the shared soul of humanity created from one soul. The psychological, social, and cultural struggle to fulfill these aspirations have helped to evolve community life for generations of common people. Shared souls evolving by the sincerity of faith under G'd, as a great Mercy shaped from the ignominious nature of the "Forest Gump" nothingness of the social and material world.

Why Use the Term Writer/Scribe/Author?
Chapter (16) Sūrat l-Naḥl (The Bees)

> "Do they not look at Allah's creation, (even) among (inanimate) things – How their (very) shadows turn round from the right and the left, prostrating themselves to Allah, and that in the humblest manner?" Al Qur'an, Yusuf Ali, S. 16, A. 48.

The term "writer/scribe" is preferred for use in this evolving series of monographs for the authorship of written works derived from the shared spirit, intellect, and many voices of the long generations of the children of Adam. The Goal? A continually evolving, universal language and logic advancing the social spirit of community life as a shared vision supporting common humanity.

As a writer/scribe working to represent the shared sentiments of a Plural Body of committed education workers, a Muslim, African

American and privileged child of Southern Segregation, this small contribution is part of the ongoing effort to promote a legacy of universals. Universals that many like me were blessed to understand and accept as a reflection of being raised in Sunday School, as were many among Muslim African Americans (even though I wasn't always paying attention). Perhaps only a few would understand the absolute blessings of such a Sunday School upbringing as still evolving in the social sentiments of Muslim-Americans professing what some may still assume to be a particular and strange brand of belief. And G'd Knows Best, and G'd Be Praised! Al humdulilahi Rabil Alamin!

The Goal?
A Unity of Universals

As an obligation of Rational Faith, the primary goal is to inform the Material and Social Sciences with the Spiritual Sciences and Scriptural Reasoning based on Al Qur'an as the source. The goal is promoting a unity of rational logic supporting the universals of other scriptures based on principled logic found in human nature, the philosophical and social constructions of most societies and cultures.

If G'd Wills, the intention for this series means only respect for all among humanity who seek Nobility & Justice for the human soul. And May G'd forgive us all as the Judge and Guide that reminds us that the clarity of common sense, simplicity and civility are precious commodities in a Man-Made world of tangled perceptions, confused motives, rational lies and deceptions that belie what we know and believe.

The paying forward of the debt with respect is a small price for help in the healing of the symptoms of the socially constructed "Cultural Insanity" created by the deconstruction of the soul spoken of in these monographs. Insanity in the collective consciousness and Plural Body of humanity is induced by artificially constructed cultural influences and spiritual and material confusion. The result of predatory self-interest, greed and what we as human beings have done mutually and continue to do. May G'd help us all against the oppression from within our own selves.

"Al Islam Linguistic or Language Construction is Most Important."

"What is alluded to is competing with those who have high knowledge, it is not only the material construction but also competing with those who have higher knowledge. We don't know that Al Qur'an reveals to us the most important construction is not the material construction it is the linguistic or language construction. It says, 'He laid the foundation of the House ,' it is talking about the Ka'bah. But what is the more appealing, more revealing, or more enlightening concept? It is not that little physical structure we're looking at." — Imam Mohammed, Warith Deen (raa), Adult Dawah, 20 March 2005, Chicago, IL. Lecture.

PART ONE
"50,000 Years!" "The End of that Road, the Exact Sciences."

Chapter One

"FORCES OF NATURE ARE BRINGING IN THE WORLD G'D WANTS."
IWDM

The following are excerpts from Imam Warith Deen Mohammed's Ramadan Sessions in 2004:

- "Please indicate that the world's timepiece is explained by Man's plan based upon his recognition of his works but not the works of G'd. The clock of G'd, the timepiece of Allah swt, is based upon — or explained upon — our recognition of the order of the natural universe. How G'd has made this universe to bear or to operate upon His Will and His plan for Mankind."
- "These are the two timepieces. And what is more important is not to know about the two timepieces. The important thing to know is that G'd is not dependent upon the world and its leaders to bring in the world that He wants for people. Natural forces are created to usher in the world that Allah swt wants for all people. Isn't it wonderful of G'd — the Loving, Generous and Merciful G'd — to give Man an invitation to work for Him saying, 'Be My servant to bring in My world?'"
- "We really need to write volumes on science or scientific theory. This also includes our perception of the life and nature of the universe itself."
- "The Qur'an descended in the night, and the time, its duration coming down to man, is as 50,000 years. Not a thousand years, 50,000 years. Now I can't keep you with me so I'm not going to try to take you down that road. I am just going to tell you what is at the end of that road, the Exact Sciences."

Adam, the Evolving Human Soul
From Spiritual Origins to Social & Material Sciences
For Building Houses With the Universals of Civilized Life, Abraham (as)

Chapter (2) Sūrat l-Baqarah (The Cow)

"He said: 'O Adam! Tell them their names.' When he had told them, Allah said: 'Did I not tell you that I know the secrets of heaven and earth, and I know what ye reveal and what ye conceal?'" Al Qur'an, Yusuf Ali, S. 2, A. 33.

Adam (as) is understood as the ongoing evolution of the shared human soul, male and female, created by G'd as the first father of the continually evolving potential of every human soul. Adam is the potential in every soul, male and female, for establishing all the G'd-given spiritual and material needs for the civilized life of humanity on earth.

Abraham (as), when understood as the Father of Reason and Faith in the continuing evolution of the human soul, is the second father. Abraham and his son Ismael (as) are the architects and builders of the House, established as a sign of the universals of guidance required for the spiritual and rational establishment of all Mankind.

An Al Qur'an as Source, Ascension-Based, Creation-Inspired Framework for Re-rooting & Unifying Knowledge, Education & the Sciences

"Scripture is given to serve life on all levels, intelligence on all levels, sincerity on all levels. Some of us are not as sincere as others. So, it is designed to serve all levels of life and the whole of life — life for the individual, life for the family, life for the community, life for the world, life for a person in a particular profession or aim in life or ambition." Imam Warith Deen Mohammed (raa)

As a renewed perspective and proposed paradigm shift as a rational approach to Social and Material and Objective Sciences, our model begins with the logic of Scriptural Reasoning, Al Qur'an as Source and the commentary of Imam Warith Deen Mohammed (raa).

An Al Qur'an as Source, Ascension-Based, Creation- Inspired Framework provides a renewed paradigm for rerooting and unifying the foundations of knowledge, education, and the sciences. These three sources define the principled logic, moral and ethical standards, and methods for advancing a critique of the epistemological origins, philosophical applications, language constructions and etymological roots of the sciences. Scriptural Reasoning is a renewed basis for constructing the language and logic of social life and culture. The principled logic of creation and original human nature that must be kept spiritually and rationally whole) should be influenced by the guidance of reason and inspired by scripture.

These universally-minded concepts are evolving among the inspired souls of the Plural Body of the descendants of American slaves who are connecting, evolving, and applying a rational approach to the sciences in ways unparalleled in "Modern" Western education, traditional Islamic education, or other cultures of the past by Allah's Mercy.

Materialism, Deconstruction & Dissembling of the Sciences

Chapter (36) Sūrat Yā Sīn

"And a Sign for them is the Night: We withdraw therefrom, the Day, and behold they are plunged in darkness." Al Qur'an, Yusuf Ali, S. 36, A. 37.

Two Excerpts from Circumcision of the Mind:

Imam Mohammed, Warith Deen (raa). *"Circumcision of the Mind."* Imams Meeting, 1997, Masjid Bilal, Cleveland, OH. Lecture.

- "Even the sciences, the so-called sciences, have been made tools of Satan. He has the knowledge locked up for his children, even in the Sciences."
- "You're going to get one, that's materialism. We are going to give you materialism, and your rational knowledge shall be false spiritualism."

The Evolution of Adam (as) the Archetypal Mind & Soul: A Post-Modern Critique of Bio-Genic Evolution

"Man is not from G'd. He's from matter. And all matter is created by G'd." Imam Warith Deen Mohammed (raa)

> **WORD STUDY**
>
> **Evolution**
>
> *From Latin*
>
> "*E* = out of" + "*volvere* = to roll" or develop by natural processes to a higher state
>
> Harper, & Liu, Etymonline.com
>
> Interpretation
>
> Therefore, the process of unrolling, rolling out or unfolding of the whole creation.

"Natural Evolution Blocked by Man's Constructions"

"When we come into the 'enlightened' world of Man, and Man learns Psychology and invents a new environment, original nature is shut out. The walls of Man's constructions shut out the lights and pure voices of nature. In a situation like that, we don't have something to provide security for us to keep us in touch with

the best of our human nature." — Imam Mohammed, Warith Deen (raa). 26 May 1991, Nashville, TN. Lecture.

> **WORD STUDY**
>
> **Deconstruction**
>
> "From the French *déconstruction* which means the process of breaking down or "taking to pieces."
>
> Harper, & Liu, Etymonline.com
>
> Interpretation
>
> "Taking to pieces "from natural processes. Therefore, deconstruction is the process of taking apart a body of knowledge.
>
> The parts of a body of knowledge can then be reassembled.
>
> in an artificial or deceptive form of the literal picture.

> **WORD STUDY**
>
> **Dissemble**
>
> **Dis = not or un+ Similis = like**
>
> From the Latin *dissimulare* meaning to "make unlike, conceal or disguise" the identity of.
>
> Harper, & Liu, Etymonline.com
>
> Interpretation
>
> Therefore, to dissemble is to "conceal, disguise" or hide, the logic, and language of reality under a false appearance.

No monkey has a mind! Man means mind as the implicit, scientific definition and description, even in the nomenclature of the phylogenetic scale, where Man is defined as *Homo sapiens sapiens*. *Homo* means alike, and *sapiens* means wise. The phylogenetic tree describing the highest evolution of the human species as *Homo sapiens sapiens* implies the necessity of establishing wisdom as the product of thinking and reason. Wisdom evolves with the universals of education, socialization, real-life experience and the Guidance of G'd.

The root of the term evolution is from the Latin *evolvere*, which means to roll or to develop by natural processes to a higher state — describing the process of unrolling or unfolding the whole of creation. We must note, however, that the processes of empiricism that produce objective knowledge do not tell us the origin or first cause of the processes of observable phenomenon in creation.

The term phylogenetic derives from the two ancient Greek words *phylon* meaning "race or lineage" and *geneia* meaning "origin or source." This bio-genetic classification scheme is based on the concept of a common ancestry for all species in creation, including Man. The concept that physical or genetic inheritance and capacity define Man and animal alike neglects the influences and logic of the archetypal spiritual roots, epigenetic effects, and metaphysical influences of the natural and social environment. Bio-genic explanations alone — without the support of metaphysical logic — are insufficient for explaining the necessary wholeness and integrity of the Sciences that support the evolution of civilized life.

For believers who follow the logical implications of Al Qur'an and other scriptures, sapience comes about in three ways:

1. The accumulation of creation-based knowledge and education,
2. Socialization and direct experience which inform the intuitive mind, common sense and intellect through life lessons learned with or without formal education as the primary tool, and

3. Scriptural Reasoning as "guidance sure" from the Creator of Man and the universe.

Psyché as Mind & Soul

> **WORD STUDY**
>
> **Mind**
>
> From the Proto-Indo-European (PIE)
>
> *"Men* = to think"
>
> Harper, & Liu, Etymonline.com

Chapter (2) Sūrat l-Baqarah (The Cow)

"Then learnt Adam from his Lord words of inspiration, and his Lord Turned towards him, for He is Oft-Returning, Most Merciful." Al Qur'an, Yusuf Ali, S. 2, A. 37.

Modern-Day scientific reasoning — based upon empirical observations and material logic — has resulted in, and necessitated, a separation from the dogma and once-cryptic language represented as Scripture over the last 500 years. The singular influences of material logic — as the only standard for defining universal paradigms for civilized progress and the establishment of the Psyché as mind and soul in creation — have altered and marginalized the evolution, perception, and useful support of the Spiritual and Social Sciences.

> **WORD STUDY**
>
> **Soul**
>
> From the Old English

> Sawol = "life, living being"
>
> Harper, & Liu, Etymonline.com
>
> Interpretation
>
> *Soul* = the archetypal entity created within each person that lives, feels, thinks, evolves and exercises will.

> **WORD STUDY**
>
> Sole
>
> *From the Latin*
>
> "*Solea* = sandal & *Solum* = bottom, ground or foundation."
>
> Harper, & Liu, Etymonline.com
>
> Interpretation
>
> The bottom of the foot or shoe, as an allusion to the two innate potentials of the soul, Reason (Fujur) and Spirit (Taqwah)

"Liberating the Community"

"The more society puts pressure on the masters of language to be more correct with their meanings or the definitions, the more we find the masters of language changing the policies and allowing us to have a different use of words." — Imam Mohammed, Warith Deen (raa). "Liberating the Community (Allah Takes Care of the Future)." June 17, 2007, Raleigh, NC. Lecture.

Chapter (6) Sūrat l-An'ām (The Cattle)

"It is He Who hath produced you from a single person: here is a place of sojourn and a place of departure: We detail Our signs for people who understand." Al Qur'an, Yusuf Ali. S.6, A. 98.

"Human Identity"
Imam Warith Deen Mohammed (raa)

"The human identity is what it is referring to. Really the word, Man, is used by us, and not Woman as such, in that particular definition. But originally, Man meant woman, too, even in Islam. That's why the Qur'an says, He created you from 'Nafsin Wahidah,' from one person. And if you read the Qur'an in Arabic, you read it very carefully, this one person was not Adam alone.

It says, '... He created from it, its mate....' Then Adam comes, and then the woman comes – distinct from each other. But originally, the word meant both male and female. So, whatever the Khalifa is, the man is not that by himself. Khalifa is male and female. Whatever Khalifa means, the man is not that by himself. It takes the woman with him. He has to become that 'Nafsin Wahidah' again before he qualifies to be the Khalifa. It takes the woman with him. You have to have two operating. Then he's the Khalifa."

"You say, 'How are you going to get a woman back into the man?' He has to be born again or has to be created by Allah with the sensitivities that a woman has. He has to have both: the male sensitivities and the woman sensitivities, if he is to be the best, the type of ruler that G'd wants for us on this earth." – Imam Mohammed, Warith Deen (raa). "Liberating the Community (Allah Takes Care of the Future)." June 17, 2007, Raleigh, NC. Lecture.

"Man is Spiritual and Expresses Himself Materially"
IWDM

"His first coming together is spiritual, but it expresses itself as material interest. But Man is first spiritual before he is any other form. When I say Man, I mean male and female, talking about the family of human beings we call Man, and this is in the English dictionary. Man means the individual male, and Man means the family of human beings, male and female. The dictionary entry will tell you that.

And that's what Allah (swt) says that He created us from one soul, both male and female. In the one soul. And He caused the soul to become two, and He mates, and He spreads from the two, all the males and females, men, and women on the earth. This is the picture that G-d gives us." — Imam Mohammed, Warith Deen (raa). "Looking For Happiness, Conceptual Wholeness (Four Sacred Conflicts)." Ramadan Session, 2002, Chicago, IL. Lecture.

"Potential, Male and Female."
IWDM

"Isn't this the same problem we have with our own selves, this sex problem we have? We can't decide whether we should be man or woman, female or male, or unisex, or what. But in our potential, we are both. And the best ruler, as I said earlier, must have both in him, the sensitivities of both in him in order to be a good ruler. Now that takes a lot of the macho out of the man, doesn't it? Well, look at your body. If you are a normal man, come up naturally and normally, that right muscle is a little stronger than that left one." — Imam Mohammed, Warith Deen (raa). "Liberating the Community (Allah Takes Care of the Future)." June 17, 2007. Raleigh, NC. Lecture.

"You Have a Male Side and a Female Side."
IWDM

"So, actually, you have a female side and a male side. But the scientists say most of your best help for your intellect comes from this [left] side and not from this [right] side. Isn't that what they say? So, the weaker side physically is the stronger side when it comes to intellectual ingenuity. And you know the beginning of the intellect for Adam didn't come until he had a wife. I'm talking straight, man, actual facts of history, of language, of scripture, etc." —Imam Mohammed, Warith Deen (raa). "Liberating the Community (Allah Takes Care of the Future)." June 17, 2007. Raleigh, NC. Lecture.

Chapter Two

From the Archetypal Soul to Epigenetic Influences on Evolution

> **WORD STUDY**
>
> **Archetype & Archetypal**
>
> *From the Greek arkhetypon*
>
> *Arkhē* = beginning, origin + *Typos* = "a blow, dent, mark, image, statue, character or general form"
>
> Harper, & Liu, Etymonline.com
>
> Interpretation
>
> *Archetype* = the first form or original pattern from which all things are created.

As a system of logic describing the Objective and Material Sciences of creation, we must also note the profoundly productive, useful influences and undeniable advances of language and logic based on empirical observation alone. Observations using the senses and faculties of thinking, reason and human imagination have produced a world of material abundance based almost entirely on the Material Sciences.

Archetypes are the original types, general patterns, and abstract forms from which the nature of all material things in creation develop. Archetypes are often used as the basis for creating Man-Made concepts, constructs, narratives, and stories that define a context or setting for characters in a story. Carl Jung uses the term to describe the universal meaning and unconscious aspects of the collective unconscious.

The heavenly garden is seen as an archetype or original state of mind. Darkness and Light are also archetypal or original states in creation. Adam and Eve are archetypes of every human person. Similarly, Luke Sky Walker and Darth Vader are universal archetypes of the hero and anti-hero in the fictional narrative of the Star Wars Saga.

The emerging Post-Modern paradigm of Scriptural Reasoning is based on evidence and experience that is understood as axiomatic. Axioms are also archetypal as original premises supported by Scriptural Reasoning that represent the logical pattern of creation, Man and Man's ability to integrate the Material and Social Sciences with support from the Spiritual Sciences.

"Man Means Mind, and Words Make People." — IWDM

To say "Man means mind, and words make people" is to say that the soul of Man, as both male and female, points us to the rationally-constructed exaggeration that misuses the language and logic of materialism to reduce the idea of Man to a physical, material and bio-mechanical object. An exaggeration that is further misused to reduce Man as mind to a superficial definition of skin by description. The influence of material constructs has also been misused to recycle logical influences in culture and social life from archetypal "lies" used to lower the spirit and thinking of some men to being governed only by animal instinct.

Man and Woman as mind are not physical beings; male and female are! Man is the first soul and the first mind, belonging to Adam, male and female. The deconstructed idea that Man is a material being only — defined as physically male or female and having only a bio-genetic origin — describes the human soul as animal by nature. Thus, the soul, the mind and behavior are deconstructed through a scheme that serves the devolution of culture, the domination of socially-constructed hierarchies and the global rule that empowers predatory material interests.

> **WORD STUDY**
>
> **Psyché & Psychology**
>
> **From the Greek**
>
> *Psykhē* = "soul, breath, spirit" + *logia* "study of"
>
> **Psychology**
>
> "1650's - The study of the soul, breath or spirit."
>
> "1748 – The study of the mind."
>
> "1890 – The study of behavior and the invisible principles that direct the body."
>
> Harper, & Liu, Etymonline.com

Chapter (2) – Sūrat l-Baqarah (The Cow)

'To Him is due the primal origin of the heavens and the earth: When He decreeth a matter, He saith to it: "Be," and it is.' Al Qur'an, Yusuf Ali, S. 2, A. 117.

The influences of Material Logic as a singular approach to the sciences are seen in the theory of biological/material evolution as proposed by Charles Darwin. Sigmund Freud's concept of the human Psyché also implies the notion that human nature is rooted in the biological/instinctive/animalistic drives of sex, aggression, and the pleasure principle.

The Sciences as Defined by Imam Warith Deen Mohammed:
1. Spiritual Sciences
2. Social Sciences
3. Material or Objective Sciences

> *"Those that came before and gave the wrong understanding in religion caused us to see the world in pieces, in division and lost the light that wanted us first to see the world as a whole, as one, Mankind as one, Man's purpose as one and also creation as one ..."* — Imam Mohammed, Warith Deen (raa). Imams' Retreat Part II, 16 January 1999. Randolph, VA. Lecture.

Materialism has advanced by the empirical method of direct observation and the measurable evidence of creation and human nature, including self-report, based on using the five senses and the faculties of thinking. However, we must note the incomplete influence of the Material and Objective Sciences, empirical observation, and measurement on the evolution of civilized life. Although incomplete as a system for making knowledge whole, Material and Objective Sciences are a profound basis for establishing material logic and the utility of material creation to benefit civilized life.

The methods and observations of Material Logic ensure neither the integrity and wholeness of the Social, Material and Spiritual Sciences nor the fulfillment of universal human needs and civilized aspirations.

Freud's notion of the primacy of sex and aggression view Man as an animal by nature with animal drives governed by the pleasure principle. As primal motives of animal life, sex and aggression are intertwined, and conflicting motives that describe deconstructed, social, and material aspirations and the most destructive achievements of Mankind. The glorification of destructive motives is celebrated in the context of socially-constructed, amoral, unethical, global cultural influences, such as perpetual war and the threat of atomic weapons. A fraudulent, conceptual deconstruction of original human nature, social sentiments and primal motives misused to undermine the integrity of Man inwardly that may yet destroy the Man-Made world completely.

These animalistic and instinctive motives are also apparent in the preeminence of the theory of Man's needs and aspirations being fulfilled by global economic and political systems such as Marx's Dialectical Materialism and predatory materialism in the extremes of Capitalism and other claims of exceptionalism, buoyed by White Supremacy. Einstein's unleashing of the elemental properties and forces of matter for the most profound misuse and genocidal abuse of Man's potential as mind is the most destructive possibility for destruction of the material world.

The Unseen (Bil Gaib)

Werner Heisenberg's formulation of Quantum Mechanics in 1925 — and what is known as Quantum Perception and its implications — presents profound contradictions to the logic of the Material Sciences. Quantum Perception seems to mark the boundary between the seen and the unseen (Bil Ghaib). These contradictions imply the existence of more principled logic requiring metaphysical assumptions as explanations of empirically-observable, measurable reality. The objective logic and phenomena of Quantum theory that govern the Empirical Sciences are, in turn, governed by unseen (Bil Ghaib), metaphysical principles that complement the present-day principles, language and system of logic of the Sciences that explain Man and the universe.

Post-Modern approaches to systems of reason, logic, social and cultural constructions must reflect the interdependence of the Spiritual, Social and Material Sciences to take Man to the next level of social, material, and spiritual evolution and to fulfill the shared need of the human soul in the evolution of civilized life.

A Post-Modern View of Evolution
From the Archetypal Soul to Genes & the Genesis of Man as Mind

> "................ G'd created he him; male and female created he them." (King James Bible, Gen. 1:27)

Rather than the mind being an "emergent property" of material principles or bio-genic processes that are not identifiable or present in the processes and mechanisms of the brain, Man is mind, as an evolving creation, ontologically and archetypally speaking. The rational and ethical utility of the mind requires the whole of our healthy spiritual and rational sensitivities, sensibilities, faculties, and the hard-earned lessons of life experience. The idea of Mankind having acquired another measure of wisdom, or sapience, has been explained by the evolution of the brain as biogenically-determined hardware and evidence confirmed by the progress of material civilization.

Twice Wise

Although still debated, the second *sapiens* in the taxonomic description of Man was recently revived to refer to modern human beings. Man's designation as *sapiens* implies mind, and the updated description of *Homo sapiens sapiens* means twice wise. The use of the singular term *sapiens* formerly suggested a subcategory of *Homo*, meaning same, based on physical differences between *Homo sapiens* and other hominids like *Neanderthals*. In fact, Carolus Linnaeus, who gave us the system for the modern classification of species, was the first to classify man as *Homo sapiens*.

The Gen (Jinn), Genius & Adam
Redefining the Fulfillment of Human Potential

Chapter (51) Sūrat l-dhāriyāt (The Wind that Scatter)
"I have only created Jinn and men, that they may serve Me."
Al Qur'an, Yusuf Ali, S. 51, A. 56.

> **WORD STUDY**
>
> **Genius**
>
> Gen/Jinn = "Spirit"
>
> Gen/Jinn = "Spirit" + ius, = "belonging to"
> "Generative power, spirit, inborn nature"
>
> Harper, & Liu, Etymonline.com
>
> Ius, = "belonging to," also related to the suffix -ious, meaning 'characterized by,' 'full of.'
>
> **Interpretation**
>
> **Innate or Inborn Spiritual Nature**
>
> Genius = The fullness of the metaphysical origin and evolution of the soul (Nafs) as expressed in the innate human potential of the spiritual nature.

Genes and genius, as bio-genic constructs referring to the biological origin of the brain, are viewed by Modern-day Material Science as the essential and only determinants of human potential, thinking and reason. Charles Darwin used the term *genius* to describe Man's exceptional abilities in the biological or physical sense, when genes, in fact, determine much more about the development of the mind than the "emergent" properties of the physical organ called the brain. Chimpanzees, who share 97-99% of the human genome, have exhibited no comparable or innately-determined potentials or "emergent" properties of mind as those of Man.

Gen means "inborn nature, spirit or natural intelligence." Rather than an exceptional quality of bio-genic inheritance, *Gen* and the Arabic *Jinn* refer to the nature of the spirit created from the fire of passions (An Nar). The passions are an aspect of human nature that must be managed by Fujur and Taqwah as the basis for evolving the soul and shared self.

The soul as self, or Nafs, evolves in three stages 1. Nafs Al Ammarah, the Commanding Self, 2. Nafs Al Lawammah, the Self-Accusing Spirit and 3. the Nafs Al Mutma'inah, the Self that is Pleased and Pleasing to G'd.

In this sense, genius can be understood as a more complete metaphysical origin and evolution of the shared soul as expressed in the fullness of the potential of Adam, the father of Mankind, created by Allah in every human being, male and female. Genius is an aspirational and evolutionary quality of spirit and thinking in the genesis of Man, from Adam to Abraham. The application of the universals of the Self that is Pleasing to G'd (An Nafs al Mutmainah) is established in the life example of the Last Prophet (saw) as Mankind evolves to become responsible for society.

Meta-Physics, Genes, Genesis & the Epigenesis of Genius

> "I'm not spooky, I'm not superstitious, I'm scientific, believe it or not. I'm scientific, but I believe in genetic life, I believe in the continuation of life through the genes, genetic life and the world of science that we live in right now, this great world of science and technology, etc. This world, too, believes in genetic life, that much of your life comes to you from the body, from the physical, biological cells of your mother and father, you get your life. And that life finds expression and reaches its consciousness in your own genes." — Imam Mohammed, Warith Deen (raa). "Genetic Memory, Community as the Focus for Life - Part II." Lecture.

WORD STUDY

Epigenesis

From Greek

Epi = on, upon, above + *genesis* = origin, creation

> Harper, & Liu, Etymonline.com
>
> Interpretation
>
> The effects of environment and experience on original nature.

Genes, genius, genetic and epigenetic memories from collective memory, experience and learning originate from and are complemented by archetypal, innately-metaphysical, principled logic that evolves human potential and the abilities that enable Man to construct, evolve and reconstruct the human self. The obligation and ability of Man to construct himself as mind sets Man apart from animals, as does the ability to master the natural and social environment, which supports the evolution of mind as Man, male and female.

The behavioral potentials of animals are bound by the biogenetically-determined, emergent properties of instinct as fixed determinants, buoyed only by Man's training. Man as mind "emerges" from the innate potentials of the soul then rises or falls from misusing and abusing the thinking and reasoning of his own innately-conscious mind. In scripture, the fall of Adam is a symbolic and allegorical telling of how Man as the innocent, first mind can be elevated or brought low into animal life, or lower than animal life, from misusing the innate potentials of the soul. The fall of Adam is reflected in repeated cycles and repeated failures, followed by the renewed progress and continual evolution of individual, social and civilized life.

How does the emergence of the term *Homo sapiens sapiens* as the definition of modern Man imply the idea of having acquired another measure of wisdom or sapience as wise humans? How can Man (male and female) be twice wise? The spirit and mind of Man become twice wise through the hard-earned lessons of lived experience, the indispensable merit of common sense, the influences of creation-inspired learning, the evolution of Social and Material Sciences and the guidance sure of revelation. Evolution begins with the innate sensitivities and sentiments of the soul and evolves with the language and logical circumstances of creation-based logic from the archetypal influences of primal culture passed on in the collective consciousness of epigenetic memories. The Post-Modern World is now emerging upon these repeated cycles of the evolution, elevation and progress of the innate, human sensitivities and tools of the human intellect.

The basic assumption of the classification system in the biological evolution of species used to define Man, were developed by Linnaeus in the 18th century. The concept underlying evolution is based on similarities and differences in physical, anatomical, racial, biogenetically-determined characteristics.

This present-day shortcoming in the logic of evolution and the Material Sciences can be traced back to the misuse of the logic in the story of Noah's ark as an archetypal plan for making most of humanity, animals, governed only by the socially-constructed classically conditioned influences of instinct and other patterns of animal behavior, rather than mind and soul as thinking and reason.

Though Linnaeus was a very religious man, his idea of the evolution of Man was used to support the bias of scientific racism that has since been discredited, thoroughly refuted and discarded by science. Linnaeus's concept of Man helped cultivate the now-discredited, "rational lie" of racial bias based on the exaggerated assumptions of bio-genetic evolution, now discarded as a social construct. Yet race has not been uprooted from the cultural influences, social sentiments, language constructions and flawed assumptions of so-called White Supremacy.

As a description of the original influences of nature, it is the primal culture of the natural world that informed and educated Father Adam, the first mind, male and female, as described in the clear guidance and rational certainty of faith, guided by the Scriptural Reasoning of the truth of assured certainty, the Haqqul Yaqin of Revelation and the logic of archetypal universals in creation.

Al Qur'an defines two innate potentials in every soul, Fujur and Taqwah, as the basis for the life of the innate, human sensitivities and evolution of the human spirit, thinking and reason. These two potentials represent the so-called "emergent properties" of reason and thinking as the ability to distinguish wrong from right. This language is the basis of Post-Modern, Scriptural Reasoning and suits the descriptive and definitive language and logic of axiomatic premises and objective constructions that support a renewed vision of modern philosophy and the Social and Material Sciences.

Chapter Three

How Heavy is the Mind?

Chapter (6): Sūrat l-An'ām (The Cattle)

"Say: 'Allah is witness between me and you; this Qur'an hath been revealed to me by inspiration that I may warn you and all whom it reaches. Can ye possibly bear witness that besides Allah there is another Allah?' Say: 'Nay! I cannot bear witness!' Say: 'But in truth He is the one Allah, and I truly am innocent of (your blasphemy of) joining others with Him.'" Al Qur'an, Yusuf Ali, S.6, A.19.

Brain Science

The mind is not the brain, and the human spirit and mind cannot be weighed! And it is not the mind of the human person, but the mechanisms of the physical organ called the brain that weigh between 3 and 3.5 lbs. The ape brain is 500 cc in volume, the human brain is about 1200 cc and the sperm whale has the largest brain of about 20 lbs. In terms of genetic determinants, the human brain is only 1% to 3% different than our close bio-genetically described hominid "relatives," chimpanzees.

Based upon similarities and differences in their physical or genetic characteristics, the female brain is, on average, 10% smaller than the male brain. However, as any female of any age and any man who has a mother or has been married for more than a few years will attest, It is neither the size nor the biological capacity, but the human faculties of thinking and the sensitive life of feeling that set the human being apart. Otherwise, as my mother would warn, please don't lose your mind!

Increases in learning are seen in changes of the connections between synapses in the brain and neural networks of synapses that form connections in the brain, that grow with learning and memory but are not dependent on innate brain size. These phenomena of brain science may be understood as a necessary influence that requires both nature and nurture, for the evolution of thinking and reason rather than bio-genetic mechanisms alone.

Thus, Lucy the chimpanzee was trained through conditioning paradigms to understand 2,000 words and use 1,000 signs, while a four-year-old child acquires over 10,000 words through everyday social interaction, imitation, and socialization. The behavior and capacity to adapt to the environment by animals is limited by instinct.

Animals may be trained with great difficulty and human effort to manifest the most basic of capacities of imaginative thinking, learning and reason. Thus, the exceptional chimpanzee among apes having been trained by Man, supports the idea that the mind is not simply a physical or biological creation, and the brain and human mind are not the same.

Man meaning mind as a distinct creation is not simply a physical or biological creation alone by nature. Male and man, Woman and female mind and brain are not the same, and the physical and metaphysical are not the same. It is the evolution of the Nafs — the Psyché or the individual and shared self — that evolves as Man meaning mind. As an axiomatic assumption our paradigm proposes that human beings, as twice wise *Homo sapiens sapiens*, are not simply the biological relatives of mammals or primates, even though we do have uncles that may act like a monkey.

The Evolution of the Psyche´ as Mind, Soul & Self (*Nafs*): A Post-Modern View for "The Day of Religion" (*Yawm ud Deen*)

Chapter (21) Sūrat l-Anbiyāa (The Prophets)

"The Day that We roll up the heavens like a scroll rolled up for books (completed), even as We produced the first creation, so shall We produce a new one: a promise We have undertaken: truly shall We fulfill it." Al Qur'an, Yusuf Ali, S. 21, A. 104.

Biochemical evolution is a process of something advancing with no explanation for its origin, purpose, or end. Its consequences are not based upon empirical or objective observation, as the basic standard of scientific evidence. Spirit and thinking — the naturally-innocent potential and abilities of reason — are the first mind of Adam, male and female, understood as one soul in both Al Qur'an and the Bible.

The human brain did not evolve entirely as a biogenic or physical entity. The incomplete theory of biogenic evolution has been misused in promoting the rational lies of racial and ethnic superiority. Thus, social constructs based upon varied assumptions of superiority are used to support the flawed idea of a multi-faceted, social hierarchy as the "sacred right" of some to rule all others and *all* human affairs.

Hierarchy is a sacred rule supported by socially-and-culturally-constructed logic and language environments that support the domination and exploitation of the innate potential of the mind and soul. Adam, Male and female, is the soul shared by the many, but dominated by the few in every facet of present-day civilized life. May Allah (G'd) forgive us all and Grant us His Mercy, protection, and guidance.

PART TWO

Scriptural Reasoning, Axiomatic Principles & Metaphysical Logic As Support For The Social & Material & Objective Sciences

WRITTEN ON 3/22/2023, SHABAN 30, 1444 AH

> **WORD STUDY**
>
> **Principle**
>
> "From the Latin primus meaning "first," "axiom," "assumption," "origin" or "source."
>
> Harper, & Liu, Etymonline.com
>
> Interpretation
>
> Original source for organizing logic language and language environments.

Chapter (6) Sūrat l-An'ām (The Cattle)

"With Him are the keys to the unseen, the treasures that none knoweth but He. He knoweth whatever there is on the earth and in the sea. Not a leaf doth fall but with His knowledge: there is not a grain in the darkness (or depths) of the earth, nor anything fresh or dry (green or withered) but is (inscribed) in a record clear (to those who can read)." Al Qur'an, Yusuf Ali, S.6, A. 59.

Chapter Four

Evolution: From Metaphysical Principles & Archetypal Nature, To Bio-Genic Processes

"We Don't Know What We Don't Know!"

> **WORD STUDY**
>
> **Metaphysics**
>
> *From Greek*
>
> "*Meta* = Beyond + *Physika* = Natural Sciences"
>
> Harper, & Liu, Etymonline.com
>
> Interpretation
>
> The Unseen Reality (Bil Ghaib) beyond the Physical or Natural Sciences.

Chapter (17) Sūratal-Isrā (The Night Journey)

'They ask thee concerning the Spirit (of inspiration). Say: "The Spirit (cometh) by command of my Lord: of knowledge it is only a little that is communicated to you, (O men!)" Al Qur'an, Yusuf Ali, S. 17, A. 85.

Because Man's objective or impersonal experience and empirical evidence are always incomplete, no rational source, no source in the observable reality, no science, philosophy, metaphysics or any other source of reason or creation-based logic can explain the nature of creation. Concrete beginnings and human perception of creation originate in the logic of abstract, archetypal, and metaphysical principles of spirit and thinking, that begin with the sensitive life of the heart. The mind as an abstract potential begins with primal motives, sensitivities, feelings of the perhaps-unmeasurable principles of spiritual life. If it were not so, we must inquire, "How much do innocence, love, inspiration, curiosity and hate weigh by the pound?"

Scriptural Reasoning — reasoning based on logically-supported, rational constructs from scriptural sources — can provide a renewed approach to all the systems of knowledge. The meta-physical principles of every faith, especially the Post-Modern reasoning (Ilm al Yaqin) from Al Qur'an as source and the universal principles of the revealed scriptures, the Bible and Torah are becoming such sources of reason.

For the believers and followers of Abraham (as) the Father of Reason and Faith, evolution is not the simple monkeying around with Material or Objective Sciences, making a monkey our theoretical uncle. The spiritual guidance of Scriptural Reasoning is required to evolve, maintain, and restore the human Psyché, male and female, to the health and wellness with which the first mind and soul were created.

Chapter (91) Surah Ash-Shams (The Sun)

> "By the Soul and the proportion and order Given to it and its enlightenment as to its wrong and its right."
>
> Al Qur'an, Yusuf Ali, S. 91, A. 7-8.

> "So, this is what we want to perceive of our original nature. And believe that G'd made us right. Our own indiscretions make us

wrong or our freedom to do our own thing and leave obedience and leave Taqwah, that is what causes all the problems. And where is that freedom given? In our Fujur. Allah (swt) according to His teachings in the Quran and our Prophet's (pbuh) teachings. He gave every human being He created Taqwah and Fujur." — Mohammed, Imam Warith Deen (raa). "Ramadan Session 2002: Looking for Happiness, Conceptual Wholeness (Four Sacred Conflicts)." 2002. Chicago, IL. Lecture.

Chapter (2) Surah Al-Baqarah (The Cow)

"Permitted to you, on the night of the fasts, is the approach to your wives. They are your garments, and ye are their garments. Allah knoweth what ye used to do secretly among yourselves; but He turned to you and forgave you; so now associate with them, and seek what Allah Hath ordained for you, and eat and drink, until the white thread of dawn appears to you distinct from its black thread; then complete your fast Till the night appears; but do not associate with your wives while ye are in retreat in the mosques. Those are Limits (set by) Allah: Approach not nigh thereto. Thus, doth Allah make clear His Signs to men: that they may learn self-restraint." Al Qur'an, Yusuf Ali, S. 2, A. 187.

Fajr & Fujur
The Dawn of Reason

"Fajr begins at dawn, the time when the spirit agrees with the rational... Now you see the word is 'Ettaqi,' it means to have that Taqwah for G'd, and Fujur can't you see Fajr in Fujur? This Fujur, this is Fajr, this is the time when the sign of night and the sign of dawn meet and form one line like two threads..." — Imam Mohammed, Warith Deen (raa). "Ramadan Session 2002, Topic: Looking for Happiness, Conceptual Wholeness (Four Sacred Conflicts)." Chicago, IL. Lecture.

From the Qur'an-based, Scriptural Reasoning point of view, the evolution of Man as mind describes the ongoing process of the development of spirit and thinking as innate and archetypal qualities of the mind. For believers, the one indispensable imperative for the integrity of the human Psyché is to nourish and maintain the soul or Nafs as it evolves with reason and faith. Reason and faith (Fujur and Taqwah) distinguish right from wrong and evolve together as consciousness of G'd in every human affair.

Spirit and thinking evolve from the first soul called Adam (as), male and female, in contrast to merely philosophical and objective reasoning evolving from exceptional qualities and biological origins only. Scriptural Reasoning as guidance sure, is yearned for by the soul and the conscious mind, created by their Maker in the best of molds (fee ahsani taqweem). Scriptural Reasoning, its axiomatic premises, logical inferences, and implications provide a complete archetypal and metaphysical context and "philosophical" keys that support the Material and Social Sciences. Metaphysical principles that support the logical constructions of Man and the epigenetic influences of culture on the natural and social environment, the evolving human Psyché and the evolution of civilized life.

> **WORD STUDY**
>
> **Axiom**
>
> "From Latin axioma = authority."
>
> Also - "Self-evident truth," "that which is thought-worthy."
>
> Harper, & Liu, Etymonline.com
>
> **Interpretation**
>
> "Self-evident authority for that which is thought-worthy."
>
> **Axioms In Geometry**
>
> Self-evident authority for measurement of everything in the earth.

Chapter (29) Sūrat l-Ankabūt (The Spider)

"Nay, here are Signs self-evident in the hearts of those endowed with knowledge: and none but the unjust reject Our Signs." Al Qur'an, Yusuf Ali, S. 29, A. 49.

As the basis of objective and principled logic in geometry, axioms are fundamental premises that support the exactness of measurement and the efficacy of logical arguments in philosophy and science. Axioms must be proven by inference, what is implied or evidence of the exactness that is observed. The fact of metaphysical reality, or the reality of the unseen, (Bil Ghaib) can be inferred from concrete reality, and — as beyond the observable and natural sciences. Metaphysical reality is self-evident even in the context of the infinitely linear nature and heuristic value of empirical reasoning, and the limitations of its objective conclusions. Simply said, we don't know what we don't know!

Therefore, we may infer that the logic of Scriptural Reasoning — freed of age-old dogma, cryptic nature, and symbolic meanings — may be used as an axiomatic context for understanding and supporting the logic of the sciences as much as philosophical reasoning. In the meantime, we may assume such in our effort to reclaim and integrate Scriptural Reasoning in service to a more complete understanding that supports the progress of the human condition, and we may also proceed on such a premise in a linear fashion until such is proven.

The lack of philosophical exactness in scientific rationales is more apparent than in the emerging influences and axiomatic assumptions of Scriptural Reasoning. The lack of empirical absolutes, as scientific evidence for first causes, the exactness of rational and moral-ethical conclusions and the final outcomes of evolutionary processes are the basis for such a logical critique.

Much of the proof of metaphysical reality is inferential and experiential, if not subject to experiment. Experiential evidence is entirely acceptable, especially in the methodology of the Social Sciences. As a subject for critical analysis, this notion of the integrity of Rational Sciences and Spiritual Sciences must be undertaken in the long-term context of perhaps 50,000 years. Based on the axiomatic context of Scriptural Reasoning of a metaphysical nature, stated rationally and logically, and hopefully by others in the near term of more varied insight and more qualified than this writer.

As a complement to merely philosophical and scientific certainty, the logic of Scriptural Reasoning can reconnect explanations for the how's, whys and wherefores of empirical evidence for conscious life. A goal pursued in service to explaining the metaphysical origin of Man as mind as a creation of the Originator of the Heavens, Earth, and all Mankind! The evolving logic and language of Scriptural Reasoning will serve the education and aspirations of common humanity and sober the aspirations of Elites.

Innate, Inherent or Inborn Sensibilities & Faculties
Mechanistic Brain Science as Deconstruction of The Soul

'1. *Instinct (or innate Faculties)* **2.** *Sentiment* **3.** *Desire* 4. *Passion* 5. **Intellect** **6.** *Reason* **7.** *Wisdom*" —*Mohammed, Imam Warith Deen (raa), "Historic Atlanta Address,"*

1975, *Atlanta, Ga. Lecture.*

Thinking Forms in Your Sentiments

"*You know, the thinking process that brings you, eventually, to understand this universe, that's what it's talking about. And the beginning of that thinking process has to be in your sentiments. It doesn't form in your rational mind first. It forms in your sentiments, in your feelings."* — Imam Mohammed, Warith Deen (raa). *"Ramadan Sessions Vol 1."* 2007. Edited by Ronald B. Shaheed.

The idea that Man as mind (Adam) begins with inherent potentials and metaphysical principles of mind and supports the concept of human evolution from sensations to sensitivities to sentiments to the senses that form the sensorium. These are inherent faculties that support the spiritual faculties of common sense , intuition, imagination and the inner senses or faculties and sensibilities of thinking and reason. Spirit, thinking, and mind are not material objects that can be directly observed and measured empirically. Spirit and thinking are evolving potentials beginning with inherent, metaphysical principles and innate sensitivities inherited genetically by every child, son, and daughter of Adam, as continually-evolving, human potentials.

The meaning of inherent, inborn, essential, permanent, or innate supports the notion of the principled logic of metaphysical sensitivities, meaning born within, as the basis of the mind's existence before self-expression and self-awareness evolve to become the awareness of conscious life, thinking and reason. In this context, the term instinct, meaning fixed within, when used to describe and define Man, must be better understood as referring to those uniquely-human faculties and archetypal possibilities that set Man apart from all animals.

> ### WORD STUDY
>
> ### Think
>
> *From the Old English*
>
> "To intend or cause to appear to oneself."
>
> "To reflect, imagine, conceive, consider, meditate or feel."
>
> Harper, & Liu, Etymonline.com

> "It has been narrated on the authority of Abi Ja'far al-Baqir (as) that G'd - Exalted is His Praise - created the Intellect. Then God ordered it to come forward, and it did. He then ordered it to go back, and it did. Then God stated, 'I swear by My Majesty and Honor that I have not created any creature dearer to me than you (referring to the Intellect), and I would not perfect anyone's intellect unless I like him. I shall enjoin others to do good and admonish others against evil due to their possessing the Intellect. Reward and punishment are given by means of the Intellect.'" — Hadith of the Prophet Muhammad (saw)

Although human instincts, instinct meaning fixed within, can be understood as animal urges in part, Man is unlike any animal, material, physical object, or machine. Some thinkers and their philosophies picture the human being as sharing animal urges or instincts as a common beginning in the bio-genic processes of evolving from animate and inanimate life.

Rather than being governed, and therefore limited by, biogenetically-determined, physiological and biomechanically-determined instincts, Man is the only creature in creation that must define himself, his nature, and his socially-constructed world through the proper application of his own moral conscience, conscious awareness, and perception of reality. Unlike animals who can only respond to their environment with instinct. Man can change the natural and social environment with the language and logic of culture. Culture in turn, will change man's spirit and thinking and even alter the physical and biological features of Man epigenetically over generations.

In order to promote the integrity and original excellence of human life (Fitrah), social and cultural narratives in every domain of social life, community life, culture and institutional establishment must support the principled logic of the inherent nature and design of innate potentials, human sensitivities, aspirations and the evolution of every human sensitivity, faculty and civilized possibility in every human soul.

Reciprocal Determinism is the idea that Man can construct language environments and cultural logic that in turn reconstruct Man as a spirit and thinker. Is there any animal that can create its own environment in service to recreating themselves? Not so much I think, or rather, not at all!

Chapter (95) Sūrat l-Tīn (The Fig)

"We have indeed created Man in the best of moulds. Then do We abase him (to be) the lowest of the low." Al Qur'an, Yusuf Ali, S. 95, A. 4-5.

Man as mind is understood as the evolution of both spirit and thinking. The ideas of mechanistic brain science imply that the mind and brain are the same. That brain and mind originate and are governed entirely by bio-genetically determined processes and capacities that "emerge" out of the material properties and mechanisms of the physical organ we call the brain. This idea supposes that Man as mind is the result of genetically determined, biological matter, bio-chemical and mechanical processes governed entirely by material properties and biological processes.

In other words, the physical organ called the brain, when also viewed as the mind, produces thinking, ideas, and concepts as its product — like a machine produces useful products by weight and physical description. In that case, we must ask that objectivist-empiricist-absolutist materialists offer us a measure of ideas and concepts, fresh or frozen, in kilos or pounds by exact weight. A fresh, 1-pound package each, of chemistry and algebra would be worth billions.

The mind as Man is not simply a bio-genetic mechanism. The higher order capacities of thinking and reason are not determined by bio-genetic processes alone. The capacities of thinking and reason set Man, male and female, apart from animals, that are governed by instinct. Thus,

The necessary influence of environment on the evolution and development of the mind can be seen in feral children who have had little or no exposure to human influences, socialization or education and never develop the fullness of their human capacities. Such failures to thrive mentally are partly due to the passing of critical periods of time that deprive the brain of necessary early experiences that govern the development of the brain for the capacities of learning and thinking. Feral children contradict the idea that the mind, and its capacities for thinking and reason, emerges solely from the bio-genic mechanisms of the brain.

An impoverished or culturally-deprived natural or socially-constructed, artificial environment deprives the brain of the formative experiences necessary to develop the mind, like the programming language required for a functioning computer. There are other examples of the mutual dependence of the human being as mind and the necessary influences of the natural and social environment for later discussion.

The Brain Is Hardware, the Heart Is the Sensitive Life

"If we separate from our human sensitivities, we become Jinn."
Imam Warith Deen Mohammed

If you have nothing but an appetite and no sensitivity, you don't have a sensitivity for what is right, what is morally right, what is correct behavior. If you don't have the right sensitivity, then how can you get the right knowledge? In our religion, without the right sensitivity, you can't get the right knowledge. I'm trying to show you the reasoning in this religion, and if you'll just listen, you will see that this teaching is best for you. It will make you a Muslim." — Imam Mohammed, Warith Deen (raa). "Ramadan Sessions Vol 1." 2007. Edited by Ronald B. Shaheed.

The brain is the hardware, the Man meaning mind is the programming. It is the sensitivities represented by the heart as innate potentials of thinking that evolve from the spiritual sensitivities. The heart and mind are mates in every human soul. What we take to heart is a defni8ng influence on evolving the faculties and abilities of thinking and reason. Thus, as believers and thinkers we should be constantly aware of the socially-constructed , cultural influences, language, logic constructions of the culture and inputs of information that form the spiritually-sensitive mind with environmentally-programmed influences. Rationally-constructed dissembled and deconstructed language are corrupt software inv programing that influence motives, emotions, and spiritual sensitivities, likes and dislikes.

The question is, "What logic, or corruption of logic, is in the socially-constructed language environment provided as guidance for the natural spirit of human passions (Hawa) and (Adam)?" Hawa and Adam form our thinking, as mates of heart and mind. Hawa is also our natural mother, understood as the socially-constructed Ummah, as community life expressing the best of culture and social influences. Our metaphoric Eve, or Ice hearted Isis, can become a lying Lilith, corrupted by the socially-constructed misinformation and rational lies of a socially constructed language environment. Hawa as the individual and social passions or can also be understood as Nephthys the lady of the house in ancient Egypt or Eve made from the rib of Adam as he slept on the Job. The individual and social passions are also called by other names in different mythologies and cultures.

The creation of Eve from Adam's rib, as told in Genesis 2:22, is not about Adam as mind, male and female, created from one soul. The rib is a symbol for a logical principle, separated from the naturally-innocent life of the passions (Eve), that can be misused as a socially-deconstructed, foster mother that promotes every extreme in social life and culture. A principle used as dry logic taken from Adam as mind when asleep his/her own knowledge body rather than woke, misused to deceive every male and female, by offering a rotten apple for every mind's eye.

Chapter Five

Language Environments, Environmental Determinism, Reciprocal Determinism.

The Soul+ Archetypal Nature + Nurture & Epigenetic Influences

"Al Islam wants you to be first alert in your rational mind and listen to what G'd says, although the heart is the doorway to intellectual development. You must first go through the door of the human heart to get into the rooms of the intellect..." — Imam Warith Deen Mohammed

Other factors that determine Man's capacity for evolving the mind are the nurturing influences of the caring or uncaring, hard-hearted influences of the self-interested Jinn of fiery "dry" logic in human nature and culture. The socially-constructed environment must respect the sensitivities and receptive nature of the innocent heart as well as the mind as the first mates, Adam and Hawa. That is to say it is not the idea of nature versus nurture but nature *and* nurture, where Man can change the environment by making use of language constructs that form the spirit, influence the sensitivities, senses and thinking. In this profound sense, "Words also Make people" sensitive or hard-hearted and insensitive.

> **WORD STUDY**
>
> **Macro-Aggressions**
>
> **Interpretation**
>
> Falsified, ideological constructs that influence social environments, the language and logic of culture, social sentiments, and perceptions that promote disrespect for the shared, human soul and the universals of civilized life.

As socially-constructed exaggerations, Macro-Aggressions and Micro-Aggressions in cultural environments disrupt the sincerity of shared social sentiments and human relationships. They also inspire aggressive behavior, personal and social conflicts, and predatory competition. Rationally-constructed lies like racism, sexism and other influences that deconstruct Man as Mind, Male and female work to the detriment of civilized life by diminishing human worth in service to dominating the shared human soul.

Freud's intertwined motives of sex and aggression, referred to as Eros (life instinct) and Thanatos (death instinct), are posited as basic motives underlying the primal origin of the human Psyché. The exaggerated misuse of sex and aggression as intertwined motives as a Macro-Aggression that fosters many Micro-Aggressions, that are the most destructive social and cultural influences on shard spirit and thinking. These motives of sex and aggression underlie exaggerated perceptions and conflicting urges that promote the extremes of passion in social and cultural conflicts, from fistfights to mob violence, lynching, genocidal war, and the absurdity of suicidal aggression in the possibility of global, nuclear annihilation.

Social conflicts have their origin in the undisciplined, unethical, and deliberate use of Macro-Aggressions to influence thinking and reason and undermine the innocent human spirit and shared social sentiment. As rationally-constructed exaggerations, these Freudian motives aim at reducing Man's cultural influences, perceptions, and behavior of both male and female as mind, to amoral, hedonistic pleasure-seeking. In that sense, consider why sexism as a deconstruction and marginalization of the feminine principle in every human soul is more corrupting of Man as mind than racism that imprisons the thinking and spirit in the falsehood of skin or other socially-constructed Macro-Aggressions! The logic of Eros and Thanatos as socially-constructed, inner conflicts reduce Man and Man's potentials, abilities, and cultural constructs to the level of Jinn and animal life. These socially-constructed, inner conflicts become a primary source of Macro - and Micro-Aggressions.

Admixtures of antithetically intertwined motives have led to the creation of an unthinkably-artificial cultural influence constructed on principles In archetypal animal life urges whose primal sources of motivation incline mankind toward s annihilation of the natural self-world, suicidal- genocide and global destruction. A psychotic complex of socially-constructed insanity that creates a variety of neurotic and psychotic spiritual and problems of influences on shared behavior and collective consciousness. Insanity that works against the primal innocence of human sensitivities, the primal urges of self-preservation and the evolution of thinking and reason.

As a primal motive, unfettered aggression prescribes a universal fate for all of humanity dictated by archetypal motives for deconstruction and domination of the mind of men in pursuit of domination of the earth. A diabolic urge that has yet to be abandoned or thoroughly discredited. May the Creator and Owner of creation and our shared soul protect us from our own selves.

Socially Constructed Language Environments

"Culture is ideas organized in a certain order. Knowledge takes certain patterns and forms certain orders." — Imam Warith Deen Mohammed

> "Everything in your environment is words speaking to your mind, forming you in the body. The books you read, the language of your parents, the talk you heard in the home, the words you heard in the streets, the physical things that you looked at and thought about, the physical things that you looked at and didn't think about are all words." — Imam Mohammed, Warith Deen (raa). "Words Make People."

> "All these things (in Creation) have acted as words gone into your mind, formed you, and they are forming you for as long as you live in this world. The process of making or forming human beings never stops. It goes on all the time. If you don't want yourself to be created in ill, bad, ugly or diseased forms, you have to get wise to the language of the environment and start selecting the things that you want to go into your mind." — Imam Mohammed, Warith Deen (raa). "Words Make People."

Environmental Determinism describes the difference between animals and Man as mind and how Man differs from the limited capacities of instinctive nature in mastering the natural and social environment. Languages are constructed with grammar, that forms sentences, narratives, linear and circular logic that is used to create language environments that form spirit and thinking. Thus, the profound implications of understanding that "Man means mind and words make people," — IWDM. Rational life evolves from the best of spiritual life, language, and logic of the environment. The evolution of the soul (Adam) begins with the original potential of spirit and thinking that must develop self-help and self-support through socialization and education. Education fosters the evolution of collective consciousness, community life, shared resources, common interests, universals of shared life, and the clarity of language and logic.

Although modern Man's intellectual achievements gave rise to mastery of Material Sciences based on objective reasoning, linear logic and impersonal evidence instead of subjective or personal experience, spiritual life evolves with the best influences of rationally informed language environments.

Objectivity and reasoning must also inform subjective, personal awareness, experience, and common sense as the original sources for education that informs, evolves, and enlightens the mind of individuals. Objective reasoning is a step toward clarity of language and logic that promotes free thinking, social responsibility for the shared soul as a Plural Body of humanity.

When the common soul is marginalized and the need for reason neglected because of socially-constructed ignorance, the imposition of dogmatic authority and the oft-misused distractions of popular culture, dominate all men and Man's world. When the need for wholistically universal education is neglected a mutually-shared artificiality, "dry" logic and the authority of mechanistic ideas and authoritarian principles come to rule the affairs of men.

The mind evolves and devolves the human faculties of thinking and feeling and sets the human being apart from animals. It is Man's innate capacity, natural sensitivity, original nature, experience, learning and life-long periods of education and accumulation of institutional memory that establish the mind as an evolving creation. The mind is the uniquely-human ability to create worlds of knowledge that support natural or artificial worlds.

Racism & Sexism as Socially-Constructed Macro-Aggressions, in the Social, Material & Objective Sciences

Chapter (49) Sūrat l-Hujurāt (The Dwellings)

> "O Mankind! We created you from a single (pair) of a male and a female, and made you into nations and tribes, that ye may know each other (not that ye may despise (each other). Verily the most honored of you in the sight of Allah is (he who is) the most righteous of you. And Allah has full knowledge and is well acquainted (with all things)." Al Qur'an, Yusuf Ali, S. 49, A. 13.

The idea of Adam as the universal soul has been falsified by the social constructions of Man as a specific type of the human soul referred to as physically male. This has been fundamental to the archetypal logic of racism, sexism and other socially-constructed, ideological and philosophical constructs that falsely color language environments. As socially-constructed influences, the exaggerated language constructions of racism and sexism are the classic examples of recycled, logic that maintains the social hierarchies and gradients of Modern-Day domination, wealth, social power, privilege, and civilized progress in both the East and West. The privileges of race and sex are primarily based upon the falsification of biological differences that color the mind with skin, mysteries of the physical form and other bio-genetic constructs that make some men artificially superior to others.

As a falsified language construction and socially-created Macro-Aggression and Micro-Aggression, racism is a language barrier of corrupt logic that wraps every Adam (Man as mind) beneath a shroud of varied hues of skin. Racism and sexism represent a barrier of logic that creates a superficially-false picture of Man, male and female. Both racism and sexism are based on superficial language constructions that wrap every human soul in the false logic of skin and physical form that continues to rob us all of our shared humanity, created as one soul, male and female. And yes, the also-mysterious, superficial male form is perceived as handsome and intelligent as Man meaning mind, as we should perceive the female as intelligent and mysteriously beautiful, while also being seen as Man meaning Adam, the first mind, created from one soul, male and female.

Adam, as Man of mind, male and female, evolves as shared humanity in our conscious life, society, and culture. Racism and sexism subvert the potential of the soul by putting the falsehood of skin and exaggerated physical form in our mind as superficial stereotypes through their socially-constructed cultural influences.

Sexism is a language construction (an Ism) that exaggerates the wrapping and unwrapping of the physical female and male forms as a logic expressing the exaggerated emphasis on the mysteries of physical form and beauty used as an artifice to color the perception of the shared soul. It is the mystery of form vs. the archetypal substance of mind that appeals to the imagination and exploits the socially-constructed image of the female when defined primarily as a sex object. Sexism and racism create a socially-constructed appeal that exaggerates and confuses the primal urge of sex with the superficial form used as a sign stimulus trigger the intertwined urges of sex and aggression. An application of Neo-Freudian Object Relations Theory that focuses on physical form and superficial appearance as the basis of attachments in human relationships rather than respect for the inherent nature of Man as mind, Adam, male and female. And yes, as a male, I am definitely a permanent devotee and supporter of keeping the forms and mysteries.

Coloring the mind with skin is oppression for every human soul! Skin belongs on the outside. The clear, uncolored, original, and innocent soul (Adam) belongs on the inside. We must all reclaim our shared humanity by reclaiming the language, logic and conscious life that is spirit and thinking, as Man meaning mind, male and female. We must redeem Adam (as) as the universally-shared humanity with clarity and truth!

The Recycled Boogey Men of Color: "Reverse Racism," "Critical Race Theory," & "DEI"

Race is not a card and there has been no reversal or systematic legalization of the attitudes and real experiences engendered by 400 years of the continually recycled social constructions of color Racism. The long-term socially constructed effects of slavery and segregation have not been reversed along lines of the entrenched color spectrum! The Plural body of humanity has no history or experience of a reversal of the socially constructed laws that empowered the sentiments, prejudice, plus power, of systematic exploitation, and barbarity of chattel slavery nor the alienation of segregation as influences on the shared human soul.

The socially sanctioned culture of chattel slavery is the only example of legally sanctioned barbarity that stripped the common soul of human sensitivities in order to reduce mankind to less than animal life. Social Constructions posed as culture wars by which both races continue to be morally and socially undermined, are represented in more subtle present-day dissembling, deflection, and recycling of unresolved prejudice. Despite decades of progress present-day socially-constructed culture wars, based on the notion of the false premises of critical race theory, and reverse racism, represent a psycho-socially constructed denial that recycles the repressed sentiments, behaviors and prejudices that underlie the subtle biases of systematic racism.

Freud & Psychosexual Theory, A Mind Full of Sex & Aggression

Contemplate the devolution and evolution of Man as mind from Darwin's biological/material concept to Marx's Dialectical Materialism, other extremes of greed and predatory materialism to Freud's concepts of human nature based on sex and aggression. And Einstein's mastery of the atom that provided Man with the ultimate capacity for employing animal aggression.

Sigmund Freud's intertwined and conflicting motives of sex and aggression have been almost completely discarded among the accepted theories of the Psyché as mind and soul. Yet their ideas remain firmly established as core influences in Modern-Day popular culture and social life and are deeply embedded in the collective subconscious and conscious behavior. The misuse of Material Science has debased "lesser men" to an animal level in service to material benefit and domination of the world of Man. The misuse of sex and aggression as the primal motives of creation and destruction are reflected in the long history of men seeking to dominate other men in service to dominating the material world. The sex urge understood as a primal motive to procreate and as we conceive all new life as the most basic of urges shared by humans and animal alike. Man as mind, male and female also conceives through the abilities and faculties of thinking and reason. The exaggeration of the primal motives of sex and aggression have succeeded in reducing Man and Man's culture to being an amoral, hedonistic pleasure seeker, rather than a thinker and contributor whose intellect, reason and wisdom contribute to human civilization.

Experience, Subjective & Objective Awareness

Personal experience understood as being spiritual and emotional is evidence of awareness also being subjective for every human soul. Thus, we must consider whether rational awareness is also merely personal and experiential. The conscious life is established by experience and shared awareness that informs the rational mind yet is not necessarily subject to direct empirical measurement. Self-report of subjective awareness as personal experience is a widely-accepted approach to the objective evidence of science, as are the self-reports of observable, empirical and objective evidence. Individuals informed by, and acting with, science begin with subjective premises and arrive at objective conclusions that are subjective in the context of theoretical interpretations of measurable data. Thus, objectivity evolves personal perceptions that are the authority and possession of the few who are masters of its empirical methods rather than spiritual and rational clarity for the common person especially when given as cryptic language rather than plainly stated.

The problem of reason being entirely detached from the sensitive life as the first and only basis of knowledge is the marginalization of the human passions of the common soul by ignorance of human nature. The disconnection and dissembling of universal knowledge, philosophy and science as preceding from the subjective to the objective has resulted in an artificial creation of the mind of common folks and elites alike. This Material Science and the influences of Popular culture often promote amoral and unethical influences. The dissembling of the universals of creation as the foundation of principled logic underlying the integrity of universal ideas and influences is the result of the absence of Spiritual Reasoning as an influence on the Rational Sciences.

One result of the socially-constructed influences of artificiality is the wide variety of socially-constructed Macro-Aggressions as ideas used to deconstruct Man as Mind like racism, sexism and other "rational lies" that result in a state of socially-constructed insanity. The beneficiaries of these socially-constructed divisions of artificial culture, language, and logic prefer keeping secrets, in service to seeking power and domination in the material earth by deconstructing the G'd-given abilities, natural, social, and cultural environments. Socially-constructed Macro-Aggressions are used as a scheme for achieving power as a regressive exercise in absolute futility for dominating the shared soul.

Chapter Six

The Evolution of Adam, Man as Mind, of Spirit & Thinking, Male & Female

Chapter (15) Sūrat l-Hij'r (The Rocky Tract)

28. "Behold! thy Lord said to the angels: 'I am about to create Man, from sounding clay from 1mud moulded into shape. 29. When I have fashioned him (in due proportion) and breathed into him of My spirit, fall ye down in obeisance unto him.'" Al Qur'an, Yusuf Ali, S. 15, A 28-29.

The logical premises of Modern-Day, bio-genetic Material Sciences depend upon the axiomatic, philosophical propositions of an empirically-based, reductionistic point of view that seeks to reduce the mind to a material, physiological and bio-genic logic of the brain. A reductionistic explanation of the brain as an evolving organ, dismisses the influences of the life of spirit (Ruh) breathed in from the social and cultural atmosphere and ignores the interdependence of subjective experience and reason on objective evidence.

It is not differences in biological capacity, brain size, mechanisms or other bio-genetic differences that determine the nature of Man as mind. It is the evolution and integrity of all the faculties of thinking and the sensitive life of feeling that evolve from the innately meta-physical, axiomatic principled logic described as the mysterious human soul that sets the human being apart from animals. The contradiction in the logical premises and aspirations of purely-objective materialism Is made clear in the phenomena of Quantum Perception as a model of cognition. Quantum Perception can neither explain what the mind is nor "prove" that the mind exists based upon empirical reasoning. Thus mind, understood only through brain science, remains an inexplicable human capacity, rather than being the same as the bio-genetic mechanistic processes of the brain.

The innate capacities of the sensitivities and original nature, lifetimes of experience, learning, life-long education, and the meticulous accumulation and sharing of institutional memory are fundamental requirements for evolving Man as mind. Mind is the ability to create worlds of knowledge that may support the evolution or devolution of artificial or socially-constructed environments that in turn evolve the human faculties or devolve the human to being into less than an animal.

The Deconstruction & Devolution of Adam as the First Mind

"What Satan actually did was undermine the human being's rational basis. He destroyed the human being's rational basis by leading him to rational lies."

Imam Warith Deen Mohammed (raa).

WORD STUDY

Devolution

"Rolling down or degeneration," the opposite of evolution.

Harper, & Liu, Etymonline.com

Interpretation

Fallen in quality to an inferior state, rationally and morally.

When contemplating Man's evolution, social and spiritual devolution from Darwin's theory, Marx's Dialectical Materialism and Freud's perception of human nature based on animalistic drives of sex and aggression, we must ask ourselves what makes them rational as logical constructions of Man meaning mind? Each theory implies that Man is a material being with animal urges, appetites and origins in irrational, Id-powered, pleasure-seeking animal nature. Einstein's theory that harnessed the ultimate power of material forces in creation has also led us to an absolute possibility of the madness of global suicide and mass extinction referred to as Mutually-Assured Destruction "MAD," the ultimate manifestation of aggression.

The intertwined motives of sex and aggression are among the most primal and archetypal of animalistic motivations repeated throughout the long history of men since Cain and Abel. Men seeking to dominate other men in service of dominating the material world with animal instincts — utilized in the design of socially-constructed, cultural environments. Influences that have reduced Man to a self-interested Jinn or animal nature rather than a contributor to human civilization. Socially-constructed Macro-Aggressions as the work of the self-interested Jinn masquerading as an angel within man! Aoouthu billahi min a Shaitan nir Rajim, and we seek refuge with Allah from Satan, the rejected enemy of every human soul.

"Truth Stands Out Clear from Error."
Al Quran, Surah 2, Ayah 256.
Chapter (2) Sūrat l-Baqarah (The Cow)

"Let there be no compulsion in religion: Truth stands out clear from Error: whoever rejects evil and believes in Allah hath grasped the most trustworthy handhold, that never breaks. And Allah heareth and knoweth all things." Al Qur'an, Yusuf Ali, S.2, A.256.

Consider how long a single human being might survive if created magically, but alone, on planet earth, as its soul owner. Consider what meaningful purpose and merit of being the sole master and beneficiary of all the riches of knowledge wealth, and the bounty that nature has to offer? How rational and spiritual would that Man of mind be, even if he could survive and prosper without others?

If the eight billion other humans presently on Earth were truly only animals, governed entirely by biogenetically-determined instincts and the socially-constructed influences of sex and aggression, how much civilized progress could a single mind make? How much satisfaction would that Man as mind — in the mold of a global ruler, king, master, pharaoh, the only "Khalifah fil Ard" (custodian of creation) or "Tarzan" living alone among the apes — enjoy in a world of animal life?

What has changed over the last 50,000 years as the primal motivation for evolving civilized life since the first caveman? Except that we now have thousands of atomic weapons, vast armies on land, sea, air, and outer space that use bullets, bombs, waves of light, sound energy and chemicals to paralyze and kill? What primal spirit, motivation and thinking have changed in the socially-constructed, shared human ethos, ethics and culture informed by the Material Sciences?

The most paradoxical of apocalyptic possibilities for annihilation of global humanity is the irony of a newly-evolving antagonist of Man as mind, created by men, known as artificial intelligence. A mechanical brain that is replacing the mind, like machines have replaced both the constructive and destructive use of muscle. An artificial mind capable of eliminating the source of the problem, i.e., artificial men with artificial thinking, artificial intelligence, artificial culture, and artificial spirits, evolved upon artificial ideas of the human soul?

What has changed in Modern-Day civilized life and human behavior in the use of brute force of a caveman that begun with a hand-held club, swung or thrown? What has changed in 50,000 years except the use of larger, infinitely-more-destructive weapons like nuclear-tipped, guided missiles? Where are the believing people who will beat their swords into plow shares? May Allah, G'd Almighty, forgive us all and grant us His Mercy, Protection, and Guidance.

PART THREE
"Ulul Al Bab"
Those Who Open The Doors To The Sciences

© 7/26/2023, SHABAN 30, 1444 AH

Chapter Seven

Opening the Doors of the Objective & Academic Sciences with Scriptural Reasoning

The Good News, Sura 78, An-Naba, Verse #19

"And the heavens shall be opened as if there were doors."
Al Qur'an, Yusuf Ali, S. 78. A. 19.

"When someone gives you information, they are either trying to free you or trying to enslave you. And that includes me!" – Imam Warith Deen Mohammed (raa)

"Pursue G'd's Creation for its Knowledge & its Sciences." Imam Warith Deen Mohammed (raa)

"If you want a more merciful society and you want a more merciful human life on this earth, pursue G'd's creation for its knowledge and its sciences. Then when you get it, you will bring comfort." – Imam Mohammed, Warith Deen (raa). "The Ascendant Nature: Mercy, Knowledge and Science." Lecture.

> **WORD STUDY**
>
> **Science**
>
> *Sci* - (skei) from the Proto-Indo-European (PIE) meaning "to cut, split, and Greek (skhizein) rend, cleave."
>
> Harper, & Liu, Etymonline.com
>
> **Interpretation**
>
> Science categorizes or breaks down the details of a body of knowledge derived from empirical evidence, objective reasoning, linear and inductive methods.

The term *Ulul al Bab* refers to those responsible for opening the doors of knowledge, which is essential to Service as Leadership, the personal obligation and responsibility for informing the masses, the believers, and the common souls of universal humanity. The pursuit of the universal principles and study of science in creation informed by revelation follows the insight of Imam Faheem Shuaibe and other thought leaders.

> "The correct Islamic protocol is that the people endowed with the requisite credibility, known in the Qur'an also as 'Ulul al Bab,' should form a Majlis and undertake the responsibility of delegation." — Imam Faheem Shuaibe

> "The members of the Majlis are not only possessed of a good, working knowledge of the explicit commands of the Qur'an and the observed practice (Sunnah) of the Prophet (saw), but are also people of understanding and insight (Ulul al Bab), alive to the sociological requirements of the community and worldly affairs in general." — Imam Faheem Shuaibe

The Application of Al Qur'an & Scriptural Reasoning as Renewed Sources of Knowledge

---

"Al Islam , linguistic or language construction is most important." — Imam Warith Deen Mohammed

"What is alluded to is competing with those who have high knowledge, it is not only the material construction but also competing with those who have higher knowledge." — Imam Mohammed, Warith Deen (raa). "Adult Dawah." 20 March 2005, Chicago, IL. Lecture.

America's Imam, Imam Warith Deen Mohammed (raa), introduced the Post-Modern World of the "Day of Religion," which is a renewed application of Al Qur'an, the life example (Uswah) of the Prophet (saw) and the universal principles of other scriptures that support the progress of reason and the Objective Sciences.

The application of the Spiritual Sciences to material life, culture and the establishment of institutions also promotes a collaborative, shura-based sharing of ideas for a Plural Body of leadership. The term "Plural Body" implies that our evolving, intergenerational vision, values, social sentiments, ideas, and work effort must be supported by everyone who follows the logic of Imam Mohammed. "Collecting the honey," is a model to be studied for sharing of ideas, establishing, and evolving culture, language environments and community life.

As students and followers, we must "all be Imam Warith Deen Mohammed," as a shared soul, spirit a Plural Body of workers evolving the vision, for model community life. Imam Mohammed (raa) was a follower of the Prophet of Allah (saw), the universal and complete model man and example of the best nature in the shared human soul.

In the Islamic tradition, this approach to leadership and social establishment is based on the example of the multi-religious, multi-ethnic community life established by Muhammed the Prophet of Allah (saw) in the Covenant of Medina. The multi-religious multi-cultural covenant, its social ethics, organization, and universal principles for civilized establishment is the example for the human soul in "Remaking the World."

"Lord of All the Systems of Knowledge"
Surat Al Fatihah

> "With G-d's Name the Merciful Benefactor, the Merciful Redeemer Praise be to G'd, Lord of All the Systems of Knowledge."
>
> Al Qur'an, Imam Warith Deen Mohammed translation , S.1. A1-2.

Systems function as units (one thing) and as parts of larger units, or greater unity, within the whole of creation. Man-made systems are also measured in units at which Man arrives by studying creation e.g., the foot, hand and other parts of the body, mind and spirit. This idea tells us we must structure our knowledge just as we see it in the design of the natural creation, and Shaitan certainly has undermined this effort by constructing artificial knowledge.

Imam Warith Deen Mohammed (raa) translates رَبِّ الْعَالَمِين (Rabil Alamin) as "Lord of All the Systems of Knowledge." The system of Creation we call the Universe (another meaning of Alamin) implies that whatever logic or system of knowledge or wisdom (Ilm or Hikmah) we see with our heart, our eyes or mind is part of the larger system of knowledge we call the Universe.

Science agrees with the definition of Imam Mohammed (raa). Science views each system as part of a larger system, whether it is a system of matter like planetary or star systems or a system of living things like cells, organs, and organ systems of the body or man-made systems like a car, airplane and computer. Systems may also be of abstract ideas, as social constructs and culture like Gnosticism, Asceticism, Hedonism. Or ideologies for governing politics and economic organization such as Capitalism, Socialism, Communism, Individualism, Materialism, etc.

The need for the future work of believers of every faith tradition in service to the Lord of All the Systems of Knowledge is to bring together the sciences in a universal vision that respects the original design and integrity created in nature and human nature. A design of civilized life and institutions that supports the abilities of the common person to contribute to the evolution of the best influences of culture and civilized life.

"Read! in the Name of Thy Lord and Cherisher..."
Chapter (96) Sūrat l-'Alaq (The Clot)

"Proclaim! (or read!) in the name of thy Lord and Cherisher, Who created - 2. Created man, out of a (mere) clot of congealed blood: 3. Proclaim! And thy Lord is Most Bountiful, - 4. He Who taught (the use of) the pen, - 5. Taught man that which he knew not." Al Qur'an, Yusuf Ali, S. 96. A. 1-5.

The first Ayat, or verses, revealed in Al Qur'an are a command from the Lord of All the Systems of Knowledge to read the signs of creation and revelation. The fourth Ayah affirms that it is the Lord of All the Systems of Knowledge who "taught man the use of the pen" for recording and preserving knowledge for establishing institutions and evolving institutional memory.

There are 21 million books in the library of Congress in Washington DC., the capital and seat of government of these United States of America. The tree is a universal symbol of how knowledge is organized to be read, recited, written, and recorded in the Social, Objective and Spiritual Sciences. The human body is a symbol of how knowledge evolves within Man as mind, male and female.

The tree that mixes good and evil is the only one in the garden from which it is forbidden to eat for the innocent spirit and potential of mind called Adam, male and female. Eating, understood figuratively as digesting knowledge, is also a reference to the capacity of the heart and mind to conceive and birth new concepts of spirit and thinking. Concept and conceive refer to the beginning of the literal processes of birth and the birth of ideas.

The physical design of the body is a symbol for how abstract knowledge is organized for ethical use and practical application. Spirit and thinking are both required for evolving human abilities and constructing the world of Man by obeying the command of the Lord of Creation and All the Systems of Knowledge. The common soul depends upon the productive life and fruit of the goodly tree that evolves from the natural world of primal culture, from which evolve the Material Sciences, social sentiments, traditional culture, language environments and rational establishment.

Man as Mind Stands Upon the Two Legs of Common Sense & Rational Sense

The physical structure and organization of the body is a sign of how the spirit and mind acquire, organize, and use knowledge. The form and organization of the tree — its roots, trunk, and limbs — are like the physical body with its feet, legs, torso, and arms. The tree, on the other hand, has no mind of its own with which to rule itself. Like the tree roots in the earth, the feet must be kept firmly on the ground, so the legs support the "trunk" of the human body as in standing up in prayer (Qiyam) to free the hands of the responsible person, (the Mukallaf). The mind must be grounded spiritually and rationally in creation to so the skill of the hands may be used to plant and harvest the fruits of our labor and record knowledge in the "leaves" of books that preserve institutional memory for educating the shard soul.

One Soul, Two Feet, & Two Legs

The form and function of the body is a sign of the abilities of the spirit and mind and represents how a body as knowledge functions as a consciously-organized whole of physical abilities, spiritual and rational logic. The body has the physical strength of arms and legs, the sensitive life of the heart in the chest and the head on top. The head is the leader and ruler over the figurative body as knowledge. The feet represent establishment in the material reality of creation, the hands represent control, and the heart represents the spiritual and emotional sensitivities of the body as knowledge.

The root word *legs* in Greek means to pick or select. From reading these signs, we can see that Man as mind uses intelligence to establish society in the same way that legs establish the physical ability to stand on two feet. Standing on your own two feet means having the support of the body as logic that establishes spirit and thinking.

The Arabic word *Rajulun* means man and shares the same root as the Arabic word *Rijlun* meaning leg. The root of the English word *intelligence* is also derived from *leg*, the Proto-Indo-European root meaning to gather, pick or choose — as in gathering knowledge and picking or choosing words as the power of the intellect. The relationship between the linguistic construction of *Man*, *leg*, and *intelligence* has persisted across languages and over time and reveals the necessity of Man as mind being established in creation by the evolution of the spirit and intellect understood as the two legs of conscious life.

Consider the metaphor of having, or not having, "a leg to stand on," which implies the need for the soles (or souls) of the feet to be kept firmly grounded on the earth so creation will inform feeling, thinking, speech, reading, writing knowledge and education have clear vision directly from creation.

Feet are also referred to as the measure of things (Qadr is power and measure), which implies seeing, understanding, and controlling knowledge both measurably and exactly and with literacy and language informed by intellect and reason. Twelve inches makes one foot, or a *ruler* and the ability to *rule* the self begins with the two potentials within the soul that establish spirit and thinking, Taqwah and Fujur.

The ability to stand on two feet and two legs is a sign pointing to the evolution of the two innate potentials of every human soul, Fujur and Taqwah, the metaphoric soles that root the spirit and thinking in material creation. Taqwah and fujur as the inherent potentials of the shared soul, or Nafs, should develop from the influences and experiences of the creation. With feet on the ground, the faculties and abilities of intelligent life and common sense give direct support to the development of spirit and thinking. Standing on our own two feet is a sign that the faculties and abilities of thinking and reason must evolve directly from the material reality of creation-based logic, and language. The abilities of the head and the sensitivities of the heart must work together as mates so Man as mind, male and female, may rule themselves with spirit and thinking.

Intelligent life must be rooted in the language and logic of creation-inspired, material reality in order to serve and advance civilized life. The innate potentials of the soul are created by G'd, Allah, the Owner of the human soul and must be established in material life as the two feet that support the intelligent life. The tree is also a symbolic metaphor for how knowledge directly from creation must be organized for educating the common person, so the original nature of the spirit and mind evolve directly from creation.

Education and socialization of the universal soul directly from creation, establishes the human spirit, that evolves thinking, reason, social life culture, the language constructions and logic of institutions to construct civilized life in accord with the command of the Lord of All the Systems of Knowledge.

"Dry" Logic
The Modern-Day Perspectives of Academics
Chapter (21) Sūrat l-Anbiyāa (The Prophets)

"Do not the Unbelievers see that the heavens and the earth were joined together (as one unit of creation), before we clove them asunder? We made from water every living thing. Will they not then believe?" Al Qur'an, Yusuf Ali, S. 30, A. 21.

In metaphysical language, water is a symbol for the inherent moral sensitivity (Taqwah) of the human soul. Academic, "dry" logic is the misuse and application of "objective" reasoning and empirical evidence without ethical guidance, moral standards, or concern for informing the perceptions that complement and empower subjective awareness and experience. Shared human sensitivities and conscious awareness of moral and ethical consequences benefit the common person and shared life. Taqwah, or G'd-consciousness, is the most useful and essential of moral and spiritual sensitivities and because Fujur establishes and supports Taqwah, and Taqwah supports Fujur.

A Model for Evolving Shura-Based Leadership, Shared Vision, Ideas & Language Environments

"The society that G'd wants us to have is a society that is protected by all of us, hence the saying of the Prophet (pbuh) in Arabic 'Yadul laaha alal jama'ah,' translated, 'G'd's Hand is on the whole people.' He doesn't control the people by one person; He controls the people by using all of them." — Imam Warith Deen Mohammed

Shura-based sharing of ideas is a ground-breaking basis for developing a Plural Body of leadership and Islamic democracy for establishing education. This approach, recommended by Imam Warith Deen Mohammed, means sharing spiritual and material concerns in circles of shared interest like a Majlis or Shura for developing and evolving language environments. A Majlis is a Plural Body established on the local, sectional, and national levels to promote every human need using Shura Baynahum, (mutual consultation) as a process that promotes the sharing of ideas and "collecting the honey."

The idea of a Majlis as a Plural Body for the sharing of ideas is implied in the language constructions of Al Qur'an. The term *Al Qawā'id* means foundation, principle, rule, sitting position or grammar as a language environment. *Jalsa* shares the root of the word *Majlis*, which means social gathering, council meeting or court. It also shares its root with *Mujalasa*, which means social exchange, and *Jullaas*, which means participants in a social gathering. *Qa'ida* and *Jalsa* also refer to the last, sitting position in prayer. — (From a shared conversation and exchange with Imam Kashif Abdul Karim).

The relationship between the words *Qawā'id*, *Jalsa* and *Majlis* tells us that language and shared logic begin a social process to evolve the wholistic principled life and logic of culture, community life, the Social, Objective and Empirical Sciences, systems of knowledge, shared vision, and the progress of civilized life.

The model community life of Medina Al Munawara, the City of Light, established by the Prophet of Allah (saw) is the example that informs the strategic approach to the establishment and evolution of community life promoted by the resourceful people and the Ulul al Bab of every sort, within and between every local, sectional and national community."

Systematizing & Evolving Language Environments

Chapter (34) Sūrat Saba (Sheba)

"And to Solomon (We made) the Wind (obedient): Its early morning (stride) was a month's (journey), and its evening (stride) was a month's (journey); and We made a Font of molten brass to flow for him; and there were Jinns that worked in front of him, by the leave of his Lord, and if any of them turned aside from our command, We made him taste of the Penalty of the Blazing Fire.

"They worked for him as he desired, (making) arches, images, basins as large as reservoirs, and (cooking) cauldrons fixed (in their places): 'Work ye, sons of David, with thanks! But few of My servants are grateful!'" Al Qur'an, Yusuf Ali, S. 34, A.12 - 13

For believers, the logic and language of Al Qur'an and related scriptures are the basis for unifying all systems of knowledge with respect for the spirit of rational faith including all philosophies, Modern-Day ideologies and the Social and Material Sciences that built the Modern World. And G'd, Allah (swt), Knows Best!

Sharing Models & Strategies of Best Practice

"There is no history of Prophet Muhammad (pbuh) sitting down for hours trying to work out how something was going to be done. (His) followers would organize and do great things without him knowing about it until he was told or... came upon it himself. They were all excited by the same fire, the community's advancement. It was their commitment to realize Islamic community life that motivated everybody." — Imam Mohammed, Warith Deen (raa). "A Community for All People." New Africa Radio, Progressions Magazine, Oct. 1985.

The education workers are seeking insight, help and understanding from the story of Solomon in Surah 34, Ayat 12-13 from the teachers and students of Arabic grammar as a key to the strategic approach to organizing, unifying, and systematizing the structure of knowledge based on the categories in S. 34,A. 12-13. Insights into the meanings of "arches, images, basins as large as reservoirs, and (cooking) cauldrons fixed (in their places)" in the story of Soloman and the Jinn will help inform the structure and organization of academic subject matter, curricula, methods, principles of instruction, and detailed lesson content to make and "keep knowledge whole."

Keeping knowledge whole as the Covenant of Abraham (as) with circular or deductive logic will help in categorizing and systematizing the details of factual information according to Al Qur'an as Source. Collecting and organizing the facts of linear logic, is confirmed by inductive reasoning that adds up the facts. This would be an excellent example of using Scriptural Reasoning that unifies ideas that are collected in linear fashion one step at a time as objective science does according to the deductive reasoning based on Al Qur'an Source. Inductive reasoning is organized into deductive or circular categories of logic with reasoning based on a central idea as the organizing the facts according to shared qualities and characteristics. This is a new approach to knowledge and keeping knowledge whole than present day philosophical reasoning.

We can all share knowledge from khutbahs, (and sermons), lesson study materials, work experience, skills, and expertise. Local communities with shared vision and systems of Al Qur'an as Source and creation-inspired language and logic are already finding ways of collaborating and sharing with each other, and Allah is the Guide.

Redefining Academics: A Potential in Every Human Soul

"There is an inherent urge in the soul that prods the intellect to want to have a more scientific and rational understanding of religious language – not the fairy-tale and kindergarten language that we have been trained to digest." — Imam Warith Deen Mohammed (raa)

The Academia' is the name given to the place where Plato met with his students. The word *Academic* from Greek refers to a grove of trees, which points the spirit and mind directly to the natural world in studying the origin of cultural life, the logic, and sciences of creation. Trees and plant life are a symbol of the growth of culture from the natural environment of creation. The Academy in this original sense has evolved as a symbolic place where socially-constructed language, reason and logic, man-made cultural environments, and institutional culture are derived, advanced and evolved in agreement with the natural world. A major problem of the last 500 years of the now Post-Modern World is Man's dependence upon reason alone, without respect for the origins of knowledge and the guidance of faith to inform the spirit, the shared soul, common sense and the capacity for reason.

Academics, as described in the Ascension level (4) Idris, as a potential in every soul, defines academics more definitively than any Modern-day theories as a potential of humanity as a Plural Body of people. The Idris level of Academics differs from the merely academic notion of, "dry" logic that built the Modern World and what is required academically for evolving the now Post-Modern World.

Much like the Pharaohs of Egypt who wore the sun on their head as a symbol of being the g'd, Ra far too many among Modern-day rulers seek an ill-gotten, figurative crown. A crown of absolute authority and power dependent upon dry logic and authoritarian leadership with an insensitive heart and dry logic, as the only way of knowing as the example for leading the Post-Modern World.

The believers in Al Islam, especially those African-American followers of America's Imam among whom "the light of rational faith is rising in the West," possess a sincere spirit and desire to contribute to the universals that will evolve the Post-Modern World. There is a great need and shared desire for psychological, social, and cultural influences and shared logic that supports the evolution of universal human aspirations for America and the global, human family, and May G'd's Peace be upon us all!

Chapter Eight

The Spiritual Sciences Support The Social Sciences & Material Sciences

Prayer of the Muslims for Jews and Christians

"'O Allah (swt), make Muhammed (pbuh) successful and the followers of Muhammed (pbuh) successful as You did for Abraham and the followers of Abraham.'

"Who are the followers of Abraham?"

"Muhammed (pbuh) knew the tendency in the people and the tricks of the world that they were going to try to separate him from Christ Jesus (as), and he said, 'Pray, O Allah, make Muhammed (pbuh) successful and the followers of Muhammed (pbuh) successful as You did for Abraham and the followers of Abraham.' So how were they made successful? Those who claimed to be followers of Abraham, many of them are, firstly, Jews.— Imam Mohammed, Warith Deen (raa). Ramadan Session. 2003, Homewood, IL. Lecture.

Keeping Knowledge Whole, the Covenant of Abraham (as)" IWDM

The Promised Land is a spiritual kingdom, and the Covenant of Abraham (as) to "keep knowledge whole" is a mandate for every believer, educator, student, preacher, and Imam. Abraham's covenant is an obligation of every faith tradition to study and promote rational establishment to educate and inform as a contribution to the evolution of the universal human soul.

Al Qur'an and other scriptural sources must inform the origins of the language of education and the sciences and that which is taught for the benefit of the social life and culture of the future of all others among As Saliheen, the righteous believing people.

Wholistic Principled Logic aims for shared ideals and ethics for universal education, as a necessary basis for redefining and unifying the foundations of knowledge. The Ascension-based framework provides a context for structuring knowledge based on narratives from Al Qur'an as Source and creation-based constructs for developing and structuring lesson content and instructional methods at every level of education.

The Ascension of the Soul is an evolving, creation-inspired framework that represents a Qur'anic paradigm for rerooting and reunifying the foundations of knowledge, the sciences and education. "Keeping knowledge whole" is among the highest of universal ideals expressed in the logic and language of Muslim, African-Americans as students, educators and resourceful followers of America's Imam, Imam Warith Deen Mohammed (raa).

The Ascension of the Soul
"Worlds Revolving Around a Core..." IWDM.
Chapter (65) Sūrat l-Talāq (The Divorce)

"Allah is He Who created seven heavens and of the earth a similar number. Through the midst of them (all) descends His Command: that ye may know that Allah has power over all things, and that Allah comprehends, all things in (His) Knowledge." Al Qur'an, Yusuf Ali, S. 65, A. 12.

"Man, Who Has to Be Responsible For Society."

> "The narratives of the Prophets (as) in the Ascension of the Soul address all of the concerns and unify concepts of revealed scripture and details of science required for establishing and evolving Man, who has to be responsible for society." — IWDM: Man, and the Universe as Mates Created for Each Other: Its Timeless Relevancy, Session # 5.

The narratives of the Prophets (as) in the Ascension of the Soul address all the concerns for unifying the concepts of revealed scripture and the details of science required for establishing and evolving "Man, who has to be responsible for society." (IWDM) The Ascension of the Soul as a Framework aims at "Aligning Two Worlds of Reality, the Social World and the Natural World." The unity of these two Worlds as interconnected environments is being studied by resourceful believers whose commitment is widely accepted in service to the cause of education and establishing community life.

"Worlds Revolving Around a Core," "Seven in Earth & Seven in Light" IWDM

> "We have to apply the light from the Ascension to the earth. There are seven tracts in the sky and seven in you, a total of fourteen. Complete 7 in earth and 7 in light." Imam W. Deen Mohammed Ramadan Session 2006, 10-15-2006, Topic: Man, and the Universe as Mates Created for Each Other: Its Timeless Relevancy, Session # 5.

"Worlds revolving around a core," as an Al Qur'an as Source concept from the commentary of Imam Mohammed, means that all of what we understand as creation and revelation descends from the Heavens by Allah's command. And the Ascension of the Soul as an Al Qur'an as Source framework provides a wholistic approach to the critical analysis of the social and cultural logic that informs the evolution of the human soul.

Imam Mohammed states the purpose as, to define "steps in the evolution of Man who has to be responsible for society." Each level of the Ascension of the Soul Framework corresponds with the ascension of the Prophet Muhammad (saw) during Al Isra' wal Mi'raj, the Night Journey and Ascension into the Heavens, and the Qur'anic narratives of the Prophets he met along his Ascension (as). The Prophets represent the prophetic, spiritual, metaphysical, psychological, social, and cultural universally shared potentials that can evolve and develop within every human soul. The Ascension of the Soul approach to education aims to evolve the human soul by providing keys from Scriptural Reasoning to inform all the spiritual, rational, and ethical concerns for promoting universals of education to evolve the shared soul in the Social and Material Sciences.

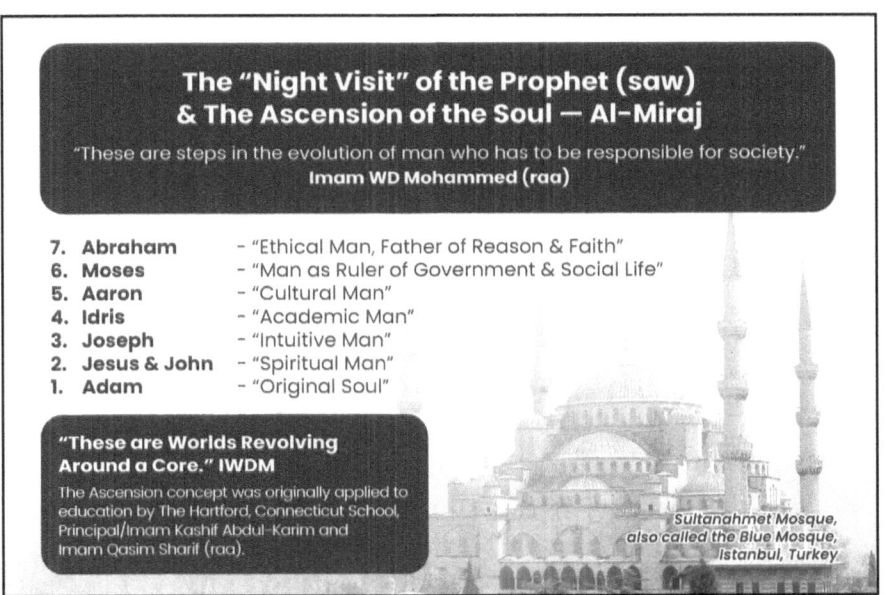

Strategic Analysis with the Ascension of the Soul Construct: Aligning Two Worlds of Reality: The Social World & The Natural World

> "And the heavens shall be opened as if there were doors."
> Al Quran, Yusuf Ali, S. 78. A. 19.

The Ascension of the Soul is a G'd-given approach to informing, planning and application to evolving the spiritual life, thinking and reason of Man as mind as the basis for efforts to educate. The Ascension evolves the human soul the natural urges of innate potential in service to constructing the language and logic of the creation-based social and cultural life that begins with Adam and establishes the rational faith of Abraham. The evolution of civilized life requires the construction of language environments of logic, ethics, and spirit to inform the past and present and plan for the future of social life and institutions.

The Imams and educators of the community of Imam Warith Deen Mohammed (raa) are sharing insights into the Ascension as a major framework for establishing education with wholistic principled logic that supports the human soul. Please share your critical insights with others in the spirit of shura-based collaboration as sharing of ideas. This aim has been defined, refined, focused, and mandated by Imam Mohammed's instructions and commentary and by those before him who sacrificed for 90 years and more for us to have this G'd-given opportunity.

Reclaiming Academics - Ascension Level 5 - Idris: A Potential in Every Human Soul

Chapter (96) Sūrat l-'Alaq (The Clot)

1."Proclaim! (or read!) in the name of thy Lord and Cherisher, Who created- 2. Created man, out of a (mere) clot of congealed blood: 3. Proclaim! And thy Lord is Most Bountiful, - 4. He Who taught *(the use of) the pen, - 5. Taught man that which he knew not." Al Qur'an, Yusuf Ali, S. 96. A. 1-5.*

"Adam (as) is the potential of every human soul from which the totality of the human potential evolves through shared effort and education for spiritual, rational, and material establishment of worlds of 'revolving around a core.'" – IWDM

The Ascension of the Soul commentary, given by Imam Warith Deen Mohammed (raa) in his 1999 lecture, is the basis for defining how every aspect and expression of the human soul develops, including as "worlds of knowledge revolving around a core." The Ascension is an integrated, wholistic conception of all issues of development as a Plural Body of humanity based on Scriptural Reasoning and establishes a context for every issue related to the evolution of Man as spirit and mind in the Social and Material world.

Speaking of the first level of development of the human soul, the Imam speaks of Adam as "the nature for that, the whole matter, holding all the possibilities for that kind of development or ascension is in the matter, G'd created it, so Adam is the first level." Adam is understood as the Father of all Mankind, and the foundation of the shared life of humanity that must include every individual self or soul to have peace on earth. The first three levels of the Ascension of the Soul — 1. Adam 2. Jesus and John and 3. Yusuf —represent movements in the Plural Body of Mankind that begin as the movement of rivers or pure, natural urges in the soul from which every individual and shared self develop. The term *Nafs* refers to the shared soul as Adam, both the individual, male and female and the Plural Body of Man as a collective self evolve. The moral sensitivities and social sentiments of the Nafs evolve as a Plural Body with the Nafs as the universal soul, Adam, and Man as both spirit and mind.

Levels 4. Idris, 5. Harun, 6. Moses and 7. Abraham are potentials within every human soul. They represent developments that begin as innate spiritual potentials on levels 1 through 3 evolving as the sensitivities that support knowledge of the self, the principled logic of creation and the ability to evolve the language and logic of culture for building and supporting institutions.

Higher education in Scriptural Reasoning and Rational or Objective Sciences, upon which the world(s) of Man evolve, becomes established in the hierarchies of education beginning at Level 4 of the Ascension of the Soul, Academics. Higher education at the bachelor's, master's and doctoral levels of the Material Sciences is usually reserved for carefully selected, privileged elites who are informed and thereby elevated above the common masses in the social hierarchy of academic, "dry" logic. Further hierarchies, sometimes secret societies and smaller circles are organized to promote esoteric, hidden, or cryptic language and logic for the symbolic "body as knowledge" of Man's worlds.

Privileged elites in turn produce the figurative "mortar" symbolized by the mortar board worn on the head in the ceremonial regalia of academia of your alma mater or foster mother. Reflect on the implications of the fact that matter and mother are from the same root word as in I. Mother Nature, II. Ummah or community life as Mother and III. Alma Mater (fostering or foster mother) refers to the institution that is responsible for your formal education. The bachelor's, master's and doctoral levels of academics have their foundational principles in the knowledge system, language, and logic of Ancient Egypt (more on Egypt later, ISA).

Archetypes, Architects, Social Engineers & Culture: Archetypal Patterns of the Human Soul

---

"G'd says that this is the religion of Fitraa, the pattern upon which He evolved human life. So, there was a pattern existing before our existence, and then G'd created us to be fitted upon that pattern. ...the whole creation is the teaching of G'd, and He created the

> *human intellect to live in that teaching environment."* — Imam Mohammed, Warith Deen (raa). Mohammed Speaks.

Shared understanding of the most ancient, archetypal influences is emerging in the evolving paradigms of Scriptural Reasoning. And Scriptural Reasoning is facilitating the increasing unity, clarity, integrity and Wholistic Principled Logic and language of the Rational and Objective Sciences.

Defining the nature of Man with socially-constructed language and logic originated with knowledge from the detailed language environment and Picto-logic of the hieroglyphics, and symbolic architecture of the temples and monuments of ancient Egypt. The monuments of Egypt can be understood as a figurative language environment and a system of logic preserved in libraries of colossal faces….and Man-Made stone.

Egypt is the most archetypal source, of original principles and understanding of the human soul among the most ancient sources of knowledge about the nature and creation of the human soul. The logic and language environment of Egypt is basic to understanding the socially-constructed, mostly-cryptic influences that shaped the now past Modern World.

Socially-Constructed Barriers of Cryptic Language & Logic

Macro-Aggressions as socially-constructed influences are used to create exaggerated extremes of logic and language as barriers to the evolution of the human soul. These include misguided, customs prohibitions, biases, traditions, and laws created at higher levels of knowledge and education. Socially-constructed barriers separate humanity according to race, gender, ethnicity, and nationality. Cryptic language and logic are a means of containing mass publics, specific groups, or people as dependents on the privileged power of socially-organized elites who manage social constructions, logic, and language environments.

The term *Matrix*, as used in the 1999 movie series title, defines a socially-constructed language environment and proverbial box of social conformity or a matrix of ideas and influences that shape the spirit and thinking. The movie series is filled with allusions to the misuse of the logic used in creating artificial environments of language and logic. Artificial environments create artificial men as minds whose spirit and thinking are influenced so profoundly, the uninformed mind and behavior can be almost completely controlled. The culture wars against "waking up" to the present day is offering America and the world the blue pill of forgetting and going back to sleep to the recycled artificial language and logic environment.

The Plural Body of the human soul, as a "Neo" type understood as a post-modern Adam (as), needs the red pill of Scriptural Reasoning to wake up to socially-constructed, artificial, falsified language environments and logic constructions. "And the light is on! "

> **WORD STUDY**
>
> Architect
>
> "Arkhi" from Latin - (Also Arch, Arc, Ark) = First or chief builder +
>
> Teks = to weave, fabricate, plan or craft and
>
> Texton from (teks) = "chief builder, carpenter, weaver,
>
> one who plans or contrives."
>
> Harper, & Liu, Etymonline.com
>
> Interpretation
>
> Builders of language environments and social constructions
>
> that begins with archetypal logic and abstract language.

"Language Construction is Most Important."
IWDM

"What is alluded to is competing with those who have high knowledge. It is not only the material construction, but also competing with those who have higher knowledge." – Imam Mohammed, Warith Deen (raa). "Adult Dawah." 20 March 2005. Chicago, IL. Lecture.

Architecture, in the abstract or metaphysical sense, refers to the systematic organization of knowledge as language and logic, as the basis for social constructions. Imam Warith Deen Mohammed (raa) made the connection between architecture and archetypal plans as the construction of buildings and the construction of the language, logic and ideas of culture. Imam Mohammed's insight is based on detailed study of Qur'anic grammar and G'd-given insight that, "Language Construction is Most Important." After all, "culture is knowledge organized in certain patterns or taking certain orders" (Imam Mohammed).

In the abstract or metaphysical sense, architect refers to all those who organize the systematic language and logic of culture and social constructions that began with the language and logic of the heavenly garden as an environment created within and for every Adam as spirit and mind. The origins of post-modern Wholistic Principled Logic must be brought into agreement with the original, Fitratullahi nature of Man as mind in original state of creation. Man as mind began in a heavenly garden without and within. The heavenly garden is a metaphoric language environment from which Adam (as) the universal soul and custodian of creation evolves, guided by the Will of the Creator, Owner, and Originator of every human soul.

The evolving construction of language environments requires open access for the common soul to higher education, language and logic that helps establish the universals of Scriptural Reasoning. Wholistic Principled Logic informs rational faith and the integrity of the Social and Material Sciences that support the evolution of culture, social life, and civilized progress. In cultures based upon the rule of privileged elites, organized in levels of social hierarchy, the mass publics of common people are influenced, conditioned, and trained to remain in their prescribed places as dependents on the socially-constructed influences, language, and logic environments of artificial culture.

> **WORD STUDY**
>
> **Elites**
>
> *E*, -Latin, = "out of" or "to bring out" + "lite"
>
> Lite, from Old English = "little or not much,
>
> also alternative for light"
>
> Harper, & Liu, Etymonline.com
>
> Interpretation
>
> Those who possess a little of the light of creation & revelation.

Chapter (24) Sūrat l-Nūr (The Light)

"Allah is the Light of the heavens and the earth. The Parable of His Light is as if there were a Niche and within it a Lamp: the Lamp enclosed in Glass: the glass as it were a brilliant star: Lit from a blessed Tree, an Olive, neither of the east nor of the west, whose oil is well-nigh luminous, though fire scarce touched it: Light upon Light! Allah doth guide whom He will to His Light: Allah doth set forth Parables for men: and Allah doth know all things." Al Qur'an, Yusuf Ali, S. 24, A. 35.

"Allah Chose Human Nature To Lead The World"

> *Then G'd says to the dry men of logic, who have all dry logic and no human nature, He says to them "yes, this unlearned human being shall become your leader whether you like it or not". Yes! That is what G'd is saying to us. That He is going to show His plans to the world. That He has chosen human nature to wear the crown of leadership on this earth. Not academic intelligence, not academic knowledge, He has chosen human nature. Not the doctors of psychology, not the economists, not the great philosopher, He has chosen human nature."* Imam W Deen Mohammed (raa)

Intellectual, social, and cultural "E-lites" are select members of academic or other socially-constructed, organized hierarchies that offer increased certainty of reason in service to would-be-absolute authority. The idea of elitism as the priviledge of a few in understanding the language and logic of culture with a "little of the light" of creation and as more than the "dry" logic of the Academic Sciences.

Yet many among the present-day elites neglect the clear light of Scriptural Reasoning that informs and supports the Objective Sciences for educating and evolving the shared human soul. The light of Scriptural Reasoning evolves with the spirit and word given to all the Prophets of G'd. Such is the light for the shared soul that is Jesus, son of Mary, who said in relation to those who believe, of his own nature and spirit, "I am in them, and you are in me !" (*New Living Translation*, John 17.23)

The universal human soul needs the light of scripture for a world that supports the potential of, the innocent original soul and Fitrah nature of Adam (as) understood as the universal human soul, male and female. The universal soul evolves from the universal nature of Father Adam (as) and is established according to the plan (Millah) of Father Abraham (as) the Father of Reason and Faith. The light of faith is guided and confirmed by the light of revealed scriptures given to all the Prophets, known and unknown.

As believers among many others, Muslims make no distinction between the Prophets, and the complete example is the last, the model man, Mohammed (saw) of Arabia, the Seal of the Prophets (as). The Prophets and prophecy are unified and completed by the book of light (AnNur) and the model example of Muhammed (saw) that clarifies guidance for all the worlds nd systems of knowledge, to establishing and evolving the Wholistic Principled Logic and ethical use of the Sciences with Rational Faith to benefit all of Mankind. The present-day culture wars and mutually-cancelling, left-wing and right-wing extremes, the diversity, equity, and inclusion initiatives and bans on teaching of history are a regressive, legal, and social strategy designed to preserve the power and domination of cultural influences and social life. A contemporary recycling of the shared spirit of common souls, both "Black and White" included, back to their prescribed places. This strategy of recycling and redesigning of cultural logic resembles a regression of progress back to the Jim Crow era, of the KKK and lynchings that followed the Reconstruction period and the later period of segregation that began to end 70 years ago with the murder of Emmet Till and Mother Rosa Parks tired feet.

Every Bird Needs Both Wings

The present-day culture wars and mutually-cancelling, left-wing and right-wing extremes, the diversity, equity, and inclusion initiatives and bans on teaching of history are a regressive, legal, and social strategy designed to preserve the power and domination of cultural influences and social life. A contemporary recycling of the shared spirit of common souls, both "Black and White" included, back to their prescribed places. This strategy of recycling and redesigning of cultural logic resembles a regression of progress back to the Jim Crow era, of the KKK and lynchings that followed the Reconstruction period and the later period of segregation that began to end 70 years ago with the murder of Emmet Till and Mother Rosa Parks tired feet.

Living Our Best Life Is Living Our Shared Life

Social Darwinism is a philosophical application of the bio-genic concept that Homo sapiens sapiens is no more than an animal. Redesigned and updated language environments of recycled archetypal conflicts are prescribed to preserve social hierarchy. An archetypal system based on the exaggerated, ideological merit of Social Darwinism as survival of the fittest in the dog-eat-dog competition of every group and individual is divided in heart and mind in service to selfish or personal self-interest. Social Darwinism is a primary construct that supports socially-constructed hierarchies and artificial language environments, in which only some dogs eat, some are enriched, and others elevated as demi-g'ds.

As elite's, town fathers in a democracy are public servants, selected to be protectors of the common worth and common good of the human soul. Yet many are as powerless as their dependents, being held in check by personal privilege in socially-constructed language environments based on hierarchies of knowledge, power, and authority. Thus, the mass public remains dependent upon the privileged, too often-self-interested, neglectful, town fathers of the extremes of left-wing and right-wing social interests.

> **WORD STUDY**
>
> **Social**
>
> (Socialize, & Socialization)
>
> From the Latin, *socius* meaning "companion or ally."
>
> Also, Sociable = join, unite.
>
> Harper, & Liu, Etymonline.com

> **Interpretation**
>
> Living with or coming together with others.
>
> Social = to bring together to form the basis of society
> Related - Ism = an ideology or system of ideas i.e., Socialism.
>
> Social, Socializing & Socialization - to bring the shared soul together as a Plural Body of humanity in light of shared social concerns.

Language deconstructions of code words such as "Socialism ," are misunderstood in spite of the fact that all human relationships are social in nature. The common masses, however, are often limited in coming together especially in circles of education. Elites are often organized in social circles of knowledge, influence, and power while common people are undermined, and remain disorganized in coming together and cooperating as participants in constructing social life. Elites come together forming think tanks, corporations and other social entities around every shared concern that supports social, cultural, political, and economic interests. Common people are trained and influenced to use only the basic skills of reading, writing, and arithmetic, and the practical applications of knowledge required as individuals and workers.

The cryptic use of code words, in the influences of social environments such as "Socialism," promotes the extremes of self-interested individualism among common people. Unlike hierarchies of socially-organized, governing elites, including corporations, the masses are kept in their prescribed places by the suggestions of language environments. Thus, mass publics become alienated, being powerless instead of being educated as thinkers and equal participants in evolving culture and building the structured life of institutions. "Yet as the children of Adam, male and female all men are created equal and endowed by their creator with certain inalienable rights."

Dividing the Mates

Chapter (2) Sūrat l-Baqarah (The Cow

"They followed what the evil ones gave out (falsely) against the power of Solomon: the blasphemers Were, not Solomon, but the evil ones, teaching men Magic, and such things as came down at Babylon to the angels Harut and Marut. But neither of these taught anyone (Such things) without saying: "We are only for trial; so, do not blaspheme." They learned from them the means to sow discord between man and wife. But they could not thus harm anyone except by Allah's permission. And they learned what harmed them, not what profited them. And they knew that the buyers of (magic) would have no share in the happiness of the Hereafter. And vile was the price for which they did sell their souls, if they but knew! Al Qur'an, Yusuf Ali, S. 2, A.102.

WORD STUDY

Individual & Individualism

'Greek origin meaning "two, double, twice,

Also, Di, PIE root *dwo - "two."

In = Old English, Inside + *divi* = divided + *dual* = Two

Harper, & Liu, Etymonline.com

Interpretation

To be divided inside in two! +

"Ism" = an idea or system of ideas

Therefore Individualism = an idea that divides the mates of heart and mind as symbols of spirit and thinking!

When the mates (Zawjain) of heart and mind are separated and deconstructed, **1.** the individual and personal life become deconstructed, **2.** family life becomes deconstructed and dissembled, **3.** the clan or extended family life is deconstructed, **4.** tribal or interest groups are deconstructed. Division within the soul produces division in and between **5.** nations and peoples or ethnic groups and **6.** every soul among **7.** Mankind as a Plural Body is deconstructed when the universal nature of the soul is lost.

The heart and mind are the first mates, as explained by Imam Salahuddin Hanif, based on Imam Warith Deen Mohammed's commentary. When the heart and mind are separated by extreme individualism as a socially-constructed influence, the spirit and mind within and the social relationships of humanity become divided on every level of expression. The myth of Cupid and Psyché is an age-old myth describing the heart and mind belonging together. The stories of Isis and Osiris, Set and Nephthys are versions from the ancient sources of Egyptian mythology of how the mates of the mind and soul, and all the mates in creation, belong together.

Education is the key to establishment of universal vision to guide the evolution of spiritual sensitivities and human motives, and emotions as the basis of thinking and reason for the common soul. In that sense universal vision must be established first, to support the spiritual faculties and abilities on Ascension Levels 1-3. Culture as ideas designed, controlled, and often manipulated by well-organized, intellectually-informed, socially-privileged elites should support this universal purpose. As civilization evolves Mass publics of every sort are also emerging to contribute to universals in the context of the practical aspects of education including by workers who apply the skills and muscle power still required of manual laborers.

The world is emerging from a modern age that began with the Industrial Revolution, that replaced the need for physical muscle power, into a world that is now replacing brain power with Artificial Intelligence. The world has too often misused the "dry" logic of academic brain power that follows the exaggerated interest of the Cain Principle to the point of exploiting the social nature and productive abilities of Abel in every child of Adam (as). A division of shared abilities of the common soul in service to self-interest that is also exhausting the resources of the natural world! The common sense and innocent spirit of Adam (as) understood as the universal soul that evolves in material reality requires a greater effort to overcome the socially-constructed barriers, rational lies and exaggerated social influences of the Post-Modern World to evolve and survive.

Who is the master architect of socially-constructed, corrupt language and logic environments that divide the soul as mates of heart and mind internally, of the common masses, social elites and leaders alike? Who is the architect of such socially-constructed, artificial language environments? Satan, the arch deceiver, and the enemy of all Mankind! And the battle is within! Aoouthu billahi min ash shaitan nir Rajim When the soul, understood as Adam, is deconstructed by the influences of language environments, the whole world of civilized progress is lost until the Creator, Owner and Originator of Creation and the soul, created (Nafsin Wahidah), forgives and restores the life of Adam, the universally-evolving, human soul! And we seek Allah's (G'd's') protection for all of Mankind from the rejected enemy in the battle within our own souls!

Chapter Nine

The Human Body as a Symbol for The Organization of Knowledge

Chapter (41) Sūrat Fussilat (Explained in Detail)

"Soon will We show them our Signs in the (furthest) regions (of the earth), and in their own souls, until it becomes manifest to them that this is the Truth. Is it not enough that thy Lord doth witness all things?" Al Qur'an, Yusuf Ali, S. 41, A. 53.

The figurative or symbolic language of the form of the human body as knowledge and its socially-constructed, philosophical and ideological implications are typically held in secret even from those with the privileged light of academic, "dry" logic. Cryptic, or hidden knowledge is used and misused by those who have influences at the highest levels of knowledge of the Sciences of Psychology, Social, Material and Spiritual Sciences in the self-interest of dominating the public life prescribed for the common soul.

Cryptic language and logic, like that found in the ancient, symbolic Picto-logic of Egypt, is used to create formidable barriers of language that keep the common person dependent upon a self-appointed few as spiritually, rationally, socially, and culturally -immature dependents.

WORD STUDY

Ankh

> The Egyptian Key of Life
>
> "Literally = Life or Soul"
>
> Harper, & Liu, Etymonline.com
>
> Interpretation
>
> "The key to knowledge, put in the head to control the person."
> IWDM

> "It is actually made to be a symbol of the human body without a head on it, that's what it's made to be. It's a ring, and it's called a key. It's a ring. You put your hand in the ring, and then the part you put in to unlock, you hold the ring and you stick the straight part in the lock to unlock it. So, it is a key, it is called a key of life." — Imam Warith Deen Mohammed (raa). (December 2, 2001). Ramadan Session III [Radio broadcast]. Masjid Taqwah. Chicago, IL.

The Ankh as a symbol of the human form represents a picture, in the figurative logic and language of myth and imagination, that shows us how cultural influences can be misused to control the human spirit, mind and behavior. There are other signs in the sciences of Egypt, like the Ankh as a key of life, that symbolize the ability to use and misuse the Psychological, Spiritual and Social Sciences to control the spirit and thinking of the common masses of people. The hidden or cryptic meanings of the symbolic logic of ancient Egypt are still used in the Modern World to control those who lack independent thinking, rationally-informed authority, self-discipline, responsibility, and independent leadership by using the headless body as a sign.

> "So, she [Isis] is holding a headless body, and what she has in her hand in Egyptian language is called the Key of Life. That key represents the science of the human Psyché, its light, what it wants, and what controls it. Because once you have the science

> *of the life of a thing you have power to control it if G'd doesn't intervene, you hear what I said? If G'd doesn't intervene, you have the power to control it."* — Imam Warith Deen Mohammed (raa). (December 2, 2001). Ramadan Session III [Radio broadcast]. Masjid Taqwah. Chicago, IL.

The circle of the Ankh is a head held in the hand with a nail projecting from it. The length of the nail represents the trunk of the body as knowledge. The lower urges and anatomy are also referred to as representing animal urges. The upper body or chest represents the social sensitivities of the heart while the lower body represents animal urges and appetites both without their own head. The body whose head is held in the hands of Isis is symbolic of a body as knowledge lacking unity, integrity, authority, and leadership. The length of the nail is also symbolic of linear logic or the logic of science. The circle held in the hand is a sign of spiritual concern, circular, wholistic or more complete logic. The head gives direction and control over the whole body of urges and appetites, spiritual, moral, social, emotional, and rational life.

How can someone put their hand in someone's head to control them? "Because words make people, and Man means mind!" The life of the person forms through the senses, and misleading social cultural influences, cryptic language, and rational lies in the uprooted, dead language of artificial language environments will create mentally-and-spiritually-dead, or sleep-walking, zombies.

When the first mind, Adam, is kept in the dark without the head as leader the appetites — the emotional and moral sensitivities of the innocent heart — can be corruptly influenced to work against the original nature and interest of the original of the soul ! Man, meaning thinking and spirit, and the idea that words make people implies that the Plural Body of the shared human soul can be "handled" or manipulated by the shared language and logic of popular culture, popular meaning for the common people as a Plural Body.

Without both parts of the soul/soles of the feet being kept on the ground, we lack the creation-inspired, intelligent life to use the skills of the fingers and hands. Without the leadership of the head, the hands have no power to control, to create, possess or control the material environment with the power or strength of the hands, because the spirit, intelligent life, and thinking are not free. The two feet enable us to stand upright, move about deliberately and free our hands. Our head and heart give direction. And legs represent the establishment of intelligent life in the material logic of creation.

Without the hands being free, we would be just like the dog on all fours — our whole potential limited and controlled by physical urges as instinct. Bound to the material earth on all fours by instincts with no fingers, thumb, or hands with which to weave, sew, hammer, nail or write. A brain without skill, directed by the spirit and thinking to build or handle what can be grasped only meant with clumsy paws. That's what your grandma's philosophical caution, "Keep your paws off my cake and ice cream" it's not dinner time meant. You might be as hungry as a dog, but you had better behave and go wash your hands first like a civilized human being with some manners, instead of following your instincts and appetites. Don't play with Granny, or you'll get a lesson for your hard head and soft bottom!

Without the authority and leadership of the head, the feet, hands, instincts, sensitive life, appetites, and urges — symbolized by the gut, heart, mind, and sacred spirit — we are without control and direction. Thus, artificial cultural environments, and their influences, create a shared ignorance of self, and a falsified idea of the Natural and the Social World.

Losing your mind, especially your common sense, is implied by the notion of being "nailed" by the exactness of an artificial language and logic environment of corrupt ideas. Or being hit on the head with the exactness of rationally-constructed, artificial influences in culture that attempt to kill natural life and thinking.

Chattel Slavery an Experiment in Crucifying Human Soul

The mind, emptied of cultural language, logic, the knowledge, spirit, and history of millennia of civilized life, as happened with the chattel slaves brought from Africa, is almost completely erased. The Psyché can then be deliberately filled with confusion of spirit and thinking while the individual person and Plural Body of people remain physically alive but socially and culturally dead.

One third or more, perhaps up to one half, of enslaved people from Africa brought to the New World were Muslim, and Africa was not the heart of darkness. And enslaved Africans were not ignorant until the plan of chattel slavery created the confusion of spirit and thinking that covered over the sensitive life and potentials of the heart and mind of both slave and master. In that sense, the Plural Body of the common people of the United States — understood as Adam — only emerged from the socially-and-culturally-constructed darkness of that original sin beginning with the 1950's freedom movements. The recent emergence of socially-constructed culture wars represents a retrenchment and recycling of the declining issues of race in social life and culture!

Socially-constructed conflicts leave the spirit and thinking under constant attack from self-interested, artificial, cultural constructs, influences and the Macro-Aggressions of artificial language and logic. Thus, the establishment and continued evolution of the soul is kept in danger of being crucified or rendered socially, culturally, and psychologically dead Artificial cultural environments and their corrupt influences create a shared ignorance of the self as a single soul, and a falsified idea of the Natural and the Social World. Thus, the symbolic logic of being "nailed" by the metaphoric exactness of artificial language logic and corrupt ideas or being hit in the head with artificial influences that neutralize, kill or "Zombify" the natural spirit and thinking.

The sciences of ancient Egypt are misused every day in the Modern World! Narrow self-interest in social life and culture continuously appeals to the sensitive and innocent heart with false ideas inscribed in language environments. Self- serving language constructions falsify the head as leadership for every soul. Aoouthu Billahir Rahman nir Rahim. We seek refuge with the Beneficent and Merciful!

Cryptic, or Hidden, Logic & Language Speaks Over the Head of Academic, "Dry" Logic

Chapter (17) Sūrat l-Isrā (The Night Journey)

They ask thee concerning the Spirit (of inspiration). Say: "The Spirit (cometh) by command of my Lord: of knowledge it is only a little that is communicated to you, (O men!)" Al Qur'an, Yusuf Ali, S. 17. A. 85.

Academic language and logic are used to construct the ideas and influences of language environments, culture, social life, and institutions at Ascension of the Soul Levels 5, 6 & 7. One of the signs of this is the mortar board of Academic regalia that forms a square turned to a point worn on top of the head in the ceremonial attire of academics. Academic regalia represents levels of achievement in the Rational Sciences developed by pursuing Academic learning at Ascension Level 4.

The levels of higher education known as the bachelor's, master's, and doctoral degrees have origins in the 40-year course of training and education required in the Temple in Man at Thebes in ancient Egypt called by the present-day Roman name Luxor! The three levels of scribes, as educated elites, of the ancient schools of Egypt were Novice, Apprentice, and Master. These :Scribes were likely the magicians, scribes or scientists that "threw down" in competition with Moses and Harun!

Artificial Language Uproots the Spirit & Word of Creation From the Logic of Culture

Chapter (20) Sūrat Tā hā

"He said: "Our Lord is He Who gave to each (created) thing its form and nature, and further, gave (it) guidance." Al Qur'an, Yusuf Ali, S. 20. A. 50.

"Connect Knowledge."- Imam Warith Deen Mohammed

"So, history says they put the dots after Muhammed (pbuh) not before. The first Qur'an has no dots. So, our English, this Western world has a symbol for 'and,' and it's just like that, it's 'Ta marbutah.' 'Marbutah' means tied, is that right? From 'Rabata,' 'Ta marbutah,' ok. So, we are to make connections, and my advice to you is don't just study knowledge. Study knowledge and try to see its relevant connections. That's the way scientists' study, and that's the way Prophet Muhammed (pbuh) taught us to study, his original, first followers. He taught them to study with the object of trying to see relevant connections." – Imam Warith Deen Mohammed (raa).

Artificial language environments are constructed by separating, hiding, or dissembling the conventional or socially-constructed meanings of language, and disconnecting the root meanings of words from the book of creation base knowledge. And cutting off the light of Scriptural Reasoning from the heavens above. Uprooting and deconstructing words from their root meanings allows for falsification of language and logic that creates exaggerated extremes, rational lies, the darkness, and confusion of artificial language environments.

Esoteric, uprooted, cryptic or hidden meanings separate imagination and intellect from creation-inspired learning, direct observation and understanding that specifies the nature and systematic organization of ideas. Ordinary dictionaries often do not give the root meanings of words nor do most classes in the Sciences, except at higher levels of education. Studying the roots of words solves the problem of cryptic meanings, dead language and logic that confuses or bypasses the clear picture that should register in imagination.

As Man's understanding of creation is always changing and evolving so are conventional meanings of language and logic. As language evolves, the revised meanings of specific words in standard dictionaries, the vocabulary of specific academic disciplines, popular culture, and slang — or "slanguage" — are updated as standards for constructing the logic of culture.

The question of whether we get the picture from a given word or not depends on the repetition of the conventional, often-uprooted, artificial meanings of a language. Meanings, especially those of code words, are often disconnected from their root meaning and from the picture that registers in imagination. Thus, artificial language constructions can make a freedom fighter a terrorist and make drugs "dope" as in good. The "N" word, too, becomes a sign of friendship and affection depending on the circumstances, who uses it and how it is said. That is why conventional meanings of language are updated yearly in standard dictionaries as language environments are recycled, refurbished and "redecorated.".

> **WORD STUDY**
>
> **Dissemble**
>
> From Latin- *dissimulare* meaning
> "make unlike, conceal or disguise."
> "*Dis* = utterly" (completely) + "*simulare* =
> To hide, conceal, disguise."

> Harper, & Liu, Etymonline.com
>
> Interpretation
>
> Dissembling means to hide, conceal, or disguise the language and symbolic logic of reality under a false appearance.

Chapter (7) Sūrat l-A'rāf (The Heights)

"He said: 'Because thou hast thrown me out of the way, lo! I will lie in wait for them on thy straight way.'" Al Quran, Yusuf Ali, S. 7. A. 16.

Dissembling of language is to sever the meanings of words from their root meanings, creating artificial ideas and rational lies that undermine knowing and understanding. Rote memory is the ability to repeat the name of something without understanding the nature, powers, utility, or the ethical or proper use of words. Rote memory of a word as name only, without a clear picture, or no picture, in imagination, as if the word is confusing or has no meaning. We often use words without knowing the true nature of the thing to which we are referring. If we cannot "get the picture" of the original meaning of a word, we cannot understand its form (Fasawwaa), systematically-organized nature, useful potential, or measurable powers (Qadr) or wisdom or guiding principles (Hudan).

Words like *man* and *male* may be falsely equated in the imagination, based upon the dissembling of material and objective evidence when the human soul Adam (as) means Mankind, male *and* female. Or when we are given the picture of man's nature through dissembling as being an animal or as slaves as 3/5 of a man as socially-constructed, conventional meanings.

Scriptural Reasoning, Academics, Language & Logic for Evolving the Spirit & Intellect & Building Every House

Chapter (16) Sūrat l-Naḥl (The Bees)

> "One day We shall raise from all Peoples a witness against them, from amongst themselves: and We shall bring thee as a witness against these (thy people): and We have sent down to thee the Book explaining all things, a Guide, a Mercy, and Glad Tidings to Muslims." Al Qur'an, Yusuf Ali, S. 16, A. 89.

The ceremonial regalia of Academics in the Western tradition were first worn in the ceremonies of the oldest universities of Europe, established in Sicily and Southern Italy during the two-hundred-forty-year rule of the Muslims. Al Qur'an was worn atop the head as a symbol of spiritual guidance that informed the rational enlightenment of the Objective Sciences and rationally-evolved faith.

For Modern-Day architects and builders of houses, understood as institutions of every sort, the academic mortar board worn atop the head has replaced Al Qur'an as a symbol. Mortar is a mixture of lime and sand used to make cement to hold together the bricks of a building. The use of mortar is a metaphor for how language and grammar constructs hold together the philosophical building blocks of the ideological "Isms" of culture.

The mortar of language and logic that begins with the Rational Sciences and the "hard facts" of empirically-measurable evidence produced by Academics can also be informed by the principles and premises of Scriptural Reasoning. A hologram is something that is whole in the sense that each part is connected in every sense with every other part. Well-informed students and followers of the language and logic of Al Qur'an consider each Ayah to be connected to all other Ayat. The idea of a "whologram " has been used by scholars of Al Qur'an to describe this assertion about the revelation of Al Qur'an.

Conventional Meanings of Language Are Man-Made & Therefore Can Become Artificial.

Chapter (16) Sūrat l-Naḥl (The Bees)

"Do they not look at Allah's creation, (even) among (inanimate) things. How their (very) shadows turn round from the right and the left, prostrating themselves to Allah, and that in the humblest manner?" Al Qur'an, Yusuf Ali, S. 16, A. 48.

Imam Warith Deen Mohammed (raa) on Word Study

"What I am giving you is more important than what Moses brought down from the mountain." — Imam Mohammed, Warith Deen (raa). "Saviors Day Lecture." 2007, Chicago, IL. Lecture.

The science of language is referred to as Language Arts. Root words, meaning the origin of words from the books of creation, give the most exact meaning and connections of meanings that are inspired by creation and Mother Nature. While the word artificial means "contrived by skill or made by Man," socially-constructed, conventional meanings are man-made reflections of imagination and therefore are changeable in nature and may thus become artificial. Thus, agreed-upon, conventional logic and language environments — whether useful or ethical, definitive, or not — can be artificial in the sense of being man-made.

When language constructions are uprooted from the root meanings of creation, a story that is untrue becomes a creative artifice. For example, by disconnecting, dissembling, and changing the conventional meanings of words that falsify the picture of Adam as Man meaning mind, a man of color becomes 3/5 of a person lacking the faculties of imagination and thinking.

A major reason for believers to always say Allah Knows Best is the fact that the meaning of words that form language environments depends on what conventional meaning and what language is used to give the picture we imagine. The uncertainty of man-made knowing as the Haqqul Yaqin of certainty that belongs to Allah Alone is also a reason based in faith for the Day of Judgement when every soul will be given its book, and nothing will be left out! As the last word of revelation Al Qur'an as Source and related scriptures that inform Scriptural Reasoning and the universals of human nature and creation can be a more definitive source of language and logic more so than traditional Philosophy as the underpinnings that inform Objective Science.

Socially-constructed meanings of language and logic given in the complex meanings of the sciences has characteristics of hidden or cryptic meanings that are seldom understood by more than a few are designed to be understood by only a few in specific, scholarly fields of study. This is especially true for the root meanings of Latin as the dead language used in the Biological and Medical sciences. By using dead languages, changing, or hiding cryptic language and reconstructing conventional meanings, social architects and engineering is made possible especially in constructing the language environments, influences, social sentiments and the perceptions of popular culture and subcultures.

Re-rooting conventional, socially-constructed meanings is an absolute necessity to correct the dissembling of language and logic. Learning inspired by direct experience from the "books of creation" and informing creation Inspired learning with Scriptural Reasoning is necessary for re-rooting edifying and making language, logic and knowledge and wisdom whole. Re-rooting language and correcting the deconstructed use of words in artificial language environments requires the method of word study, the language and logic construction recommended by Imam Mohammed (raa). Understanding the best meaning and use of language truly is more important than "what Moses brought down from the mountain."

Meeting Places # One
High Places

Come seeker.......from Olduvai, step up yonder....
High...up places, craving the sun....
Four days climb....off......the weary road
Up the Mountains of the Moon,
Where ... the Mother....of All Mankind
And the Pharaohs descended,
Draped in myth and primeval clouds...
Beginning the journey...
To greet.........the Jesus man,
.......At the Super Wal-Mart.

Taste.......the first read,
Bursting.........
The pristine....double vault,
Of blue-green creation,
Painting consecrated logic,
On the barren.... unmeasured globe
And man-made faces.......of colossal stone.

Come seeker......
Cross Ice bound Elysian Fields, Alph de' heuze...
Down the Ganges, the Mekong, the Mississippi.
Descend from Chi Ho Drang, Machu Pichu,
On peaks of sharp clouds.
Climb down....upon the mists....of Kilimanjaro.
To the gardens....rivers flow beneath
The meek.........shall inherit.

Come thirsty traveler………
From Buktu's well,
Shake the date palm…swaying high…hhhh….
On a breeze…………an eternity of peace.
Part….the swift running rivers
With the muse of a G'd given staff.
Pray…the children of knowledge,
Will shun…….the black hearted glare,
Of their self-serving blindness.

Come seeker,
A mere step…. 10,000 years….
Up the weary road,
To the joining……of twin forks
Where Shawnee, Chickasaw….Choctaw and Cherokee
Built up …sacred mounds,
Open and high toward the sun.
Be the witness….that the Great Spirit,
Gave no claim…to the wicked will of men.

Come….from every bottom rung,
Of global mega cities
Quench your double thirst,
At the waters of Zam-Zam,
In Biblical "Shur"
Nurture the seed….that is the common soul………
By its Master's Will ……

Come traveler, of Olduvai,
Off the longgg……. weary road
Up the mountains of the Moon

To the LAST day ruled....
By wickedly – blind men.
Where the mountain....... and Muhammed (saw),
Will meet the Jesus man (Pbuh) ......at the Super Wall Mart.......
One step further.......................up the weary road!!!!....

A-Hameed El Amin ©3/28/98

In Language Construction, the Picture is the Word!

"Imagination is more important than knowledge."
Albert Einstein

Chapter (95) Sūrat l-Tīn (The Fig)

"By the Fig and the Olive, And the Mount of Sinai, And this City of security,-" Al Qur'an, Yusuf Ali, S. 95, A. 1-3.

Surat At-Tîn (The Fig) refers to the role of imagination and science in the establishment of civilized life. The fig is symbolic of imagination, and the olive is symbolic of science as understood from the commentary of Imam Warith Deen Mohammed. Imagination is picture language, or *Picto-logic*, worth a thousand words that register in the mind. If you don't get the picture in imagination from a word, especially the root of the word, you do not understand the meaning of the word.

If you don't get the complete Picto-logic from a narrative constructed with words you don't understand the logic of the philosophy, ideology or socially-constructed "Ism" either. The Ayat of Al Qur'an can re-root, inform and evolve the laws discovered by Objective Science with Scriptural Reasoning and the A, or signs of creation, with the logic of Social and Material Sciences. The language of Scriptural Reasoning is an evolving approach to the primary objective of making knowledge whole with Wholistic Principled Logic that re-roots, integrates and elevates the spirit and mind.

Unlike most languages, English is based on root meanings from multiple, other languages. These root languages include the ancient, 3rd millennium BC Proto-Indo-European languages of the Indus Valley, Latin, Germanic, Celtic, Arabic and others. Latin is a dead language that, while no longer spoken, remains the basis of the root meanings of Anatomy, Physiology, Biology, Medical and Biomedical and other sciences.

Picture language, or Picto-logic, a concept given by Daniel Mujahid, is the first language and logic from direct experience and creation. Creation-inspired, root meanings that begin with direct observation and the study of creation are the basis for Man-Made, conventional understanding. A clear understanding of socially-constructed, conventional meanings must be taken directly from, and connected to, the picture of specific things in imagination as the Picto-logic symbols of ideas, ideologies, and philosophies. In turn, pictures arise from memory and imagination as they are connected with socially-constructed, agreed-upon, conventional meanings of words assumed to be descriptive, definitive and exact in spite of being socially-constructed.

A Thousand Words for An Apple?

The picture and Picto-logic that forms in imagination with the repetition and direct experience of the senses and forms connections between words and things in creation is called *figurative language*. The picture of an apple in the imagination is associated with the conventional meaning of the word *apple* in English.

We have heard that a picture is worth a thousand words. There are 2,500 varieties of apple grown in the United Sates and 7,500 varieties across the world. For the owner of an apple orchard there are more than a thousand words required to produce the different varieties of apples. How many words are needed to describe the apple of your eye?

Apple   =

Figurative language gives the Picto-logic of the form, shape or nature of the information, idea or thing that registers in the imagination. The French *la pomme*, the German *apfel* and the Arabic *tuffah* are different, socially-constructed words for the picture of the thing called *apple* in the English language. Therefore, words in other languages can conjure the same, or very similar, pictures in the human imagination. This principle also applies to using and misusing synonyms — or meanings that are dissembled, deconstructed, and falsified — as the meanings of words to create artificial language environments. We should all revisit the story of Eve and the apple for a clear understanding through the study of Al Qur'an and the commentary of Imam Warith Deen Mohammed (raa).

Chapter Ten

"Aligning Two Worlds of Reality, The Natural World & The Social World."

The Separation of Modern Philosophy & the Rational Sciences, From the Dogma of Religion

Chapter (29) Sūrat l-'Ankabūt (The Spider)

"The parable of those who take protectors other than Allah is that of the spider, who builds (to itself) a house; but truly the flimsiest of houses is the spider's house; if they but knew." Al Qur'an, Yusuf Ali, S. 29, A. 41.

Every house, building and institution begins with the language constructs of architects who design the logic and exact language, for every structure of cultural and social life with the Spiritual and Rational Sciences. The constructions of grammar make every system of ideas and every socially-constructed language environment meaningful and coherent like mortar holds together the blocks or bricks of a building. The metaphoric idea of mortar is symbolic of the logic of grammar that connects, binds, holds together and makes meaning of language and logic.

The language constructions of architects and engineers are used to construct all the Man-Made tools, devices, machinery, and materials for every construction of civilized life. The logic of the academic sciences is laid out in the design of the cultural influences of popular culture and institutional culture like building blocks laid upon the foundation of the physical house. Foundations of language and logic establish material progress, social and civilized life in every house as an institution built to contain the accumulated knowledge, material logic, social spirit, and wisdom of civilized life.

Social Engineering

The academic, ivory-tower logic of the objectively "pure" sciences allows for the cultivation of the earth with material logic that produces wants and needs, goods and services, the power of money, social establishment, power, and systems of logic to manage the benefits of material productivity. Social engineers use the blueprints of language, logic, and culture to build the institutions of civilized life designed by architects. Engineers also build all the Man-Made tools, devices, materials, and machinery for constructing civilized life including the software and hardware of computers with artificial intelligence that is now competing with human intelligence. Engineers and social engineers can also deconstruct, disassemble, reverse engineer, or tear down and redesign their own constructions.

The Modern World places exaggerated emphasis on predatory material interest, based on the Cain Principle that supports predatory materialism at the expense of the abilities of Abel who represents the shared interest in social life. The Cain Principle represents a fixation and regression of the three natures of the self: the Jinn, Adam the Man, and the mate of the Man, Hawa, the natural passions that fell from heaven together into the struggle to evolve on the earth by Allah's permission.

This archetypal, psychological, and social fixation and regression devolves from an urge to dominate the **shared** soul for material interest by means that represent a Modern-Day, archetypal Cain Principle that has never evolved out of the ego-regressed selfish motives of the

Iblis nature, "I am better from Him." Thus, Modern-Day social life and culture remain incomplete when devolving without the G'd-given universal abilities of the common soul (Abel) to construct the world that G'd intends for Mankind!

Revelation (Wahy) from Scripture & (Wahy) From the Book of Creation

> "Educated professionals are to translate language to benefit the common man's productivity." — Imam Mohammed, Warith Deen (raa). "Ramadan Session." 2005. Lecture.

The practical purpose of this work is to help evolve the Rational Sciences that enable Man to build all the houses of civilized life. "Wahy" is a word referring to inspiration from both creation and revelation, seen as two books or sources of knowledge in agreement with and confirming each other. Scriptural Reasoning is the understanding of inspiration from creation and the guidance of revelation for making use of the Material and the Rational Sciences to support the plan for constructing every House.

Houses of Worship provide models for every man-made institutions including 1. Education, 2. Culture and Entertainment, 3. Business and Economics and 4. Government and Politics. These socially-constructed institutions support human life and are understood as houses with obligations that begin with the family, home, individual and community life that evolve to become community life, culture, and civilized life as institutions that support the civilized life of the whole human family.

Al Islam rejects the pursuit of useless knowledge. In that sense, Al Islam is a practical religion that is about what should be done more than what should be studied. Every sign (Ayah) from Qur'anic Sources of Scriptural Reasoning should be studied to inform the G'd-given, creation-inspired logic (Ayat) as guidance sure for establishing the shared obligation to individual and community life. Wahy, as inspiration from creation guided by revelation, can support the evolution of every human soul understood as Adam (as), male and female, in the construction of culture, institutions and institutional memory that continues to evolve in the "Day of Religion."

The Ka'bah, the Universal House & Universal Language Environment

> "Now, let us look at the Ka'bah, There is a sign there. The knowledge is there, ancient knowledge. If you look at the Ka'bah, you will see that it is a square. And if you look at the place where you go around, it is a circle. There is a square sitting in a circle, meaning your material conscience should be surrounded and it should be protected by 'Taqwah' (G'd-Consciousness). G'd wants us to have material consciousness, but He wants us to be protected by Taqwah." — Imam Mohammed, Warith Deen (raa). "Symbolic Language." Imam W. Deen Muhammed speaks from Harlem, N.Y. 1984, Harlem, NY. Lecture.

The journey of a lifetime, Hajj, represents the evolution of the soul as a Plural Body evolving from the original potential of Adam to meet the responsibility entrusted to Man as a Plural Body of Abraham for planning, designing, and building the institutions of civilized life. Hajj is to be performed by every Muslim who can afford to do so as the last obligation of the principles of faith. The Ka'bah, and the rituals of Hajj are signs for the complete education of spirit and mind required to construct a world that pleases G'd. The Prophet Muhammed (saw) followed the Millah (way) of Abraham (as) in performing the rituals of Hajj.

The Millah of Abraham represents a plan for evolving language, logic and the social and cultural environment that supports Man as spirit and thinking for establishing the universal human soul, male and female. The common soul must be established for the Plural Body of Mankind as participants in evolving the wholistic systems of sacred, secular, scientific, social, and cultural logic and language that begin with the archetypes of creation established in the heavenly garden(s) called Eden.

The fact that the Last Prophet (saw) followed Abraham (as) in performing the rituals of Hajj is very important to ponder as an insight into understanding the connections between the ritual obligations of Hajj, the Guidance of Al Qur'an and the life example of the Prophet of G'd (saw).

PART FOUR
Wholistic Principled Logic as Support for The Academic or Rational Sciences

© 7/26/2023, SHABAN 30, 1444 AH

Chapter Eleven

Principled Logic for "Keeping Knowledge Whole, the Covenant of Abraham"

Whole, Holy, Wholly & Wholistic Language & Logic

"Allah (swt) says in the Qur'an there are many keys. To what? To the skies, the heavens, and the earth, 'Wal ard.' The Qur'an says, '...with Allah are the keys.' If you understand it, access to the keys is made possible by Revelation. So, with the Qur'an we can have access to the keys to the skies and the earth. And with those keys, then we unlock the treasures, and then they render their yield to us.

Now, here, if we understand it, the Qur'an and Muhammed, belong together, the Word and G'd's purpose on earth and Man's life belong together, don't they? They must be reconciled. They must be brought together so that Man and the Word of G'd, which is also the spirit of G'd, the inspiration of G'd, come together in one." — Imam Mohammed, Warith Deen (raa). "Liberating the Community (Allah Takes Care of the Future)." June 17, 2007. Raleigh, NC. Lecture.

"Give that to Mankind, female and male, all nations, give that to them, then that word in Man, in a material body, will have the same effect on our possibilities for our life that the sun has on the dead earth, for the possibilities of life on earth. And we see what the sun has done in time. It has just grown life all over the earth,

> *life from the lowest level to the highest. That's Man...the most complex. That's Man."* — Imam Mohammed, Warith Deen (raa). "Liberating the Community (Allah Takes Care of the Future)." June 17, 2007. Raleigh, NC. Lecture.

Whole, holy, and wholly represent a unity of spiritual, rational and ethical concerns. Wholeness is completion in both spirit and thinking. It is a more complete idea of what is "sacred" than what is articulated by Scriptural Reasoning or the Objective Sciences alone. In our evolving language constructions based on Scriptural Reasoning, we are reclaiming "holy" as a term that means spiritual and rational wholeness that evolves from the nature and potential of Adam (as) as a single soul, male and female. The Principled Logic of Wholeness is the basis for evolving all human needs and aspirations. Thus, rather than implying a simple idea of spiritual "purity" as the standard for defining human identity, social constructs, ethnicity or describing specific people; Wholeness is completion and integrity in every aspect of Man's potential.

The evolving, Al Qur'an as Source, Ascension-Based, Creation-Inspired Framework provides a renewed paradigm for re-rooting, unifying, and evolving the foundations of knowledge, the sciences and education. The Ascension of the Soul commentary is an essential tool for categorical organization of the sciences in unifying the structure of knowledge, related academic subject matter, curriculum structure, methods, principles of instruction and detailed lesson content to Keep Knowledge Whole, as the Covenant of Abraham (as).

To articulate the principled logic of a whole or wholistic model of knowledge for constructing the language and logic of the sciences, culture, and institutions; we must consider all aspects of human nature and spiritual, natural, social, and cultural influences on thinking and behavior including those influences implied in the concept of "holy." Complete awareness of the Spiritual Sciences, Social Sciences and Objective or Material Sciences is essential to evolving the Plural Body of Mankind. Similarly, genius — understood as the fullness of awareness for which every soul is intended — implies the application and integrity of all the sciences that support human nature.

Scriptural Reasoning is essential for language construction and deductive logic to redefine and unify the foundations of knowledge and evolve the principled logic of universal education. Qur'anic logic, scriptural sources and universal principles must inform the origins of education, curriculum lesson content and social life and culture of the future for Muslims and other believing people. The Ascension-Based framework provides a complete context for structuring, knowledge based on Al Qur'an as Source, and Creation-Inspired narratives for developing a categorical approach to knowledge.

The Creation-Inspired framework is based on organizational principles that avoid the dead-end results of dogma as scientific, social, and scriptural absolutes. Dogma of every sort is a tool for asserting absolute authority in service to authoritarian dominance, exploitation and enslavement of the thinking, spirit, and reasoning of every human soul! Man-Made reason and absolutes enslave the spirit and thinking of Man as mind.

As Scriptural Reasoning is regarded as being revealed directly from G'd through the angel of revelation, it is also regarded as independent of Man's authority and philosophical reasoning. The implication is that reasoning based on scripture as a source of knowledge can be understood as objective in nature in the sense that man is not arriving at conclusions based on subjective reasoning and only arriving at conclusions that he already believes when tested empirically.

"The Mountains' Means 'Wise, Informed, Above Small Visions..." IWDM.

"The mountains' means 'wise, informed, above small visions.' It is way up and has broad vision, way up like the eagle. He goes way up, and he has a broad vision. Mountain is broad vision!" — Imam Warith Deen Mohammed (raa)

According to the Holy Bible, after the last supper and prayer in the garden of Gethsemane, with his disciples, Christ Jesus, son of Mary, was crucified on top of a mountain called Golgotha, which means *skull* in Aramaic. Moses received the ten commandments on Mount Sinai in Egypt. The Prophet Muhammad (saw) received the first revelation in a cave on the mountain called Jabal an Nur or Mount Nur, meaning the *mountain of light*. The place where the rituals of Hajj are completed east of Mecca in Arabia is called Mt. Arafah, the Mount of Mercy. This is the mountain where millions of Hajjis stand on the lowest of the seven heavens on earth, the Adam level of paradise, as a sign of the Day of Judgment when all of humanity will stand together.

The symbolic logic and language of mountains is also used in the Qur'anic narrative in Suratul Baqarah, Ayah 260, the story of the four rivers, four birds and four mountains given for Abraham's understanding as symbolic representations of how the dead are resurrected. Mountains symbolize being wise, informed and above the small visions as understanding that begins as rivers or urges in the human soul for establishing the four domains of institutional life and the universals that support social and cultural progress.

Each of these references to mountains in scripture, established as symbols of creation on the earth, also refer to what is taking place in the inspiration, elevation, evolution, and support of revelation for the human mind and soul. The G'd-given destiny and potential of the universal soul, Adam (as), in becoming "wise, informed and above the small visions," is to become the custodian of creation despite all the schemes of Satan, the enemy of Mankind!

Epistemology/Etymology
"Study from the Root of Knowledge."
IWDM

Chapter (87) Sūrat l-a'lā (The Most High)

Glorify the name of thy Guardian-Lord Most High, Who hath created, and further, given order and proportion. Who hath ordained laws. And granted guidance; " Al Qur'an, Yusuf Ali, S. 87, A. 1-3.

WORD STUDY

Epistemology

Epi = "on, upon, above + *sta* from

histasthai (PIE) = to stand"

Also, from the Greek *epistasthai* =

to know.

Harper, & Liu, Etymonline.com

Interpretation

To stand upon and study

the roots of knowledge.

Epistemology is the study of the roots of the knowledge that supports the axioms of metaphysics, philosophy, and science to prove and distinguish "justified belief from opinion" (Mohammed). Metaphysics should include the unseen reality of axiomatic or self-evident "authority for that which is thought worthy" (Mohammed). Scriptural Reasoning as the basis of a Post-Modern approach to a renewed vision that supports empirical evidence is a more valid, objective approach to the Social and Material Sciences than Modern Philosophy.

> **WORD STUDY**
>
> Etymology
>
> *Etymon* = "true sense, real,
>
> original or actual + *ology* = study of"
> Harper, & Liu, Etymonline.com
>
> Interpretation
>
> The study of the true or real sense of a word

Study the Nature of All Forms, Language & Logic
Chapter (20) Sūrat Tā Hā

> "He said: 'Our Lord is He Who gave to each (created) thing its form and nature, and further, gave (it) guidance.'" Al Qur'an, Yusuf Ali, S. 20, A. 50.

The insights for applying Sūrat Tā Hā to the study and research of every subject is proposed by Imam Faheem Shuaibe as the following:

- Study the names (nature), origins and histories of concepts, events, places, people and their origins and the connection with the logic of Creation. We may study how concepts and ideas are formed, beginning with the word study (etymology) method given to us by IWDM to understand the origin of the names of all forms in any language.

- Word Study is studying the origin or etymology of all words and informing their meanings with the constructions of Qur'anic Arabic grammar. Including all the names, systematic logic, and concepts in English to understand and follow the logic by:
  1. Studying how Allah (swt) created (khalaqa) everything in creation
  2. Studying the form (fasawwaa) as the nature and systematic organization
  3. Studying the powers and measure (Qadara) of the things in creation
  4. Studying the (Hudan) as guiding principles, logic, and ethics of name and number in all the "created things" and their connection with the unitary logic of Creation called the Universe.

This method follows the logic of Surah 20 Ayah 50 and Surah 87 Ayat 1-4. This logic can be followed in the context of studying the language or logic construction of any subject by using the grammar of Al Qur'an as the standard. For further study, see the book "***The Reality of Our Sacred Nature: Our Origins and Our Destiny* by Imam Faheem Shuaibe."**

Rote Memory, Training & Repetition, Create Spirit Without Meaning & Understanding

"Modern-Day," Western educational foundations and resources represent a material worldview of creation and human nature based on Man's reasoning alone. The language of modern philosophy and science has been uprooted from Creation-Inspired sources of learning. Thus, the foundation of social, cultural, and political ideologies is supported by material logic without support from Scriptural Reasoning, which undermines the universal social spirit and intellect.

Rote memory means the ability to repeat the name of something without understanding its nature, powers, utility, ethical or proper use despite knowing its name. Rote memory is the result of training that inputs information while neglecting to bring out the picture registering in imagination or the potentials of thinking and reason. Rote memory can be seen in the two-year-old that is trained to repeat words like "Dada" for every male person rather than a specific man who is the child's father.

Words give us pictures, and the picture we get depends on the root meaning of words. Coded or cryptic language constructions can hide or change the picture of agreed-upon, conventional meanings of language representing falsified meanings of the nature of things. Rote memory allows us to remember and repeat a socially-constructed idea or name of a thing without knowing the nature of that thing. For example, we are trained through imitation, identification, and repetition to use the term "public servants" for elected leaders whose actual behaviors and attitudes make them the self-important, selfish beneficiaries of shared life as masters rather than servants of the public interest.

The idea that *male* and *man* are the same is a result of not understanding Man as mind, rather than male, and not understanding that the female is also Adam (as) as both a spirit and mind by nature. So, too, are Black and White qualities of every mind and soul rather than skin as races of people whose minds and spirits have been falsely colored by artificially-constructed experiences and the language and logic influences of socially constructed environments.

Even more pointedly, most Modern-Day, artificial, incomplete, or falsified language environments and systems of knowledge are detached from the Fitratullahi of original creation and human nature. All sources of knowledge should be rooted in creation, but most of the language constructions of the now Post-Modern World are detached from the Spiritual Sciences and uprooted from creation. The re-rooting of the languages of the Rational Sciences is essential for informing, guiding, and correcting the ethical use and application of language and logic to all of Man's construction and ethical use of the Social and Material Sciences.

Creation-Inspired Constructions of Language Environments

Chapter (36) Sūrat Yā Sīn

37. "And a Sign for them is the Night: We withdraw therefrom, the Day, and behold they are plunged in darkness." Al Qur'an, Yusuf Ali, S. 36, A. 37.

The science of studying word origins, etymology, is essential in language construction.

Creation-inspired knowledge begins with the root meanings, language, and logic of all the forms and organized systems of symbolic language concepts and the logic of the sciences of material creation. The study of word origins is most important because every day, agreed-upon, conventional meanings begin with root meanings not usually found in ordinary dictionaries for everyday usage in popular culture and education.

The names of things in creation are derived from and point to the knowledge of the systematic form and nature of the thing, its powers and the wisdom implied by its practical and ethical use. Creation-inspired methods are cutting-edge approaches to language construction as a method for re-rooting, renewing, applying and evolving the science of linguistics and constructing all aspects of language environment. The work of Sister Nuurah Muhammed (raa) and that of other notable Imams, resourceful believers, and students of Imam Warith Deen Mohammed (raa) is contributing to a renewed body of Qur'anically-informed Scriptural Reasoning.

"Education in Creation"
Nuurah Amatullah Muhammed, MAT, (raa)

"For the human soul, 'Education in Creation' must begin as the lifelong pursuit of the knowledge represented in the 'Tree of Knowledge' so that human perceptions, understanding, and wisdom are rooted directly in Creation. Thus, through education laid in the early years of schooling, we become wise adults capable of achieving anything that we can conceive in our minds by the Grace and Will of Allah." — Nuurah Amatullah Muhammed (raa)

The work of Sister Nuurah A. Muhammed (raa) has established a basic principle that governs the origins of all forms of language construction. Sister Nuurah Muhammed's work began in service to education at the table, and by the direction of, the Honorable Elijah Muhammed. Sister Nuurah's work has shown us that five forms in creation are the basis upon which all symbols of spoken and written language are to be read, including the languages of measurement:

Five Forms in Creation
1. a vertical line,
2. a slanted line, or horizontal line,
3. an arc or curved line,
4. a circle and
5. an ellipse or oval.

The five forms described in the work of Sister Nuurah A. Muhammed (raa) are the basis for constructing the root of all language constructions of the literacy and logic used in every science including geometry, number and alphabet construction, the basic skills of reading and writing and all of the Sciences and Philosophy, including pictographic and figurative language and the symbolic language of rituals. Scriptural Reasoning based on a higher understanding of Al Qawā'id — the construction of sentences with correct grammar — is the foundational principle for evolving Wholistic Principled Logic for constructing every type of language environment and Man-Made, material creation.

An understanding of scripture rooted in Haqqul Yaqin — the highest form of language as guidance from the Lord of All the Systems of Knowledge — can inform the building of material things, beginning with every word in every book for every architect and engineer and building every house of institutional establishment. Wholistic Principled Logic informed by the "Truth of Assured Certainty" can inform every word of every form of language construction for establishing institutional memory that supports the evolution of civilized life and progress.

Satan Colors the Spirit & Mind with Skin, Crawling in the Dust of Surface Language

> *"Satan was cast down and told to do what? 'Bite the dust. Crawl on your belly. That's where your problem is, in your stomach.' So, what you're going after is going to pull you down upon your stomach, and you are going to have to crawl on your stomach. Your stomach will be your legs."* — Imam Mohammed, Warith Deen (raa). Ramadan Session, 2006. Lecture.

The esoteric meaning of crucifixion is to put to death, and artificial ideas, language and logic are used in Satan's attempt to kill the natural spirit, mind and understanding of the human soul. Hidden language and cryptic logic have also been misused to construct artificial, cultural influences and social scripts. What does crawling on the belly say about the mind? It says that the appetites, or lower urges, control what's in the spirit and thinking because they are no longer standing upright in creation with direction from the authority of their sensitive heart and head. Imam Warith Deen Mohammed states that the appetite to dominate others is the worst of all appetites.

Satan lies in wait in artificial language environments, attempting to keep the potential of Adam, the soul created from dust, from evolving. He creates rational lies and exaggerations that make skin, or other physical descriptions, a false identity that defines the soul as animal potential instead of as Adam (as), male and female. Satan's schemes attempt to keep Adam in the dust of socially-constructed ignorance, darkness, and corrupt influences to prevent Adam from becoming a competitor in industry, productive material life and civilized progress.

Socially-constructed narratives also labeled enslaved peoples with the false identity of having no human soul and being biologically and racially inferior, while giving the masters a disposition of superiority that justified the totally-immoral corruption and cruel and inhumane motivations, incentives and practices of chattel slavery. These socially-constructed, cultural attitudes used skin as a symbol for the human soul and created a rationally-corrupt spirit, mentality and exactness of socially-constructed exaggerations that enslaved all alike, deceiving the mind with false, social and cultural constructions and socially-constructed language influences.

Racism, sexism, and other social, cultural, and ideological Macro-Aggressive constructs use artificial, cultural language and logic, like skin and gender, as defining Man as mind to create socially-constructed narratives designed to influence, corrupt, or kill the G'd-given, natural, human spirit. Thus, the spirit, word, perception, and capacity to think, feel and behave morally and ethically, of both enslaved and master, die in the socially-constructed influences and corrupt sentiments of "rational" lies and language environments like chattel slavery.

Rationally-constructed exaggerations are used in an attempt to crucify Man's natural, spiritual disposition and to control the mind with influences that falsify the spirit and mind. Rationally-constructed exaggerations attempt to nail the hands and feet with the exactness of figurative language and the logic that falsely colors the soul as "Black" or "White" in social scripts of skin identity that dictate every human disposition and behavior. In a word, the heart and mind, trained in such language and logic environments, become the mental and spiritual slaves of false logic and artificial, cultural constructions that make skin a symbol for human nature painted as good or evil, superior, or inferior. We become animals with the surface language of skin!

Race is Not a Card!

There are 400 years of history of attempting to crucify the spirit and mind with the Macro-Aggressive language influences of chattel slavery and race in service to accumulating material wealth and power at the expense of the shared human soul. Thus, the mind of the chattel slave and slave master alike were stripped of the natural spirit and thinking of Man as mind. The enslaved as well as the masters were dehumanized as unwitting servants and mutual victims of the enemy of the human soul who constructs the artifices of every form of slave life. The honest and sincere soul of every nation, tribe and people among Mankind should ask a serious question about the misuse of the most sacred of obligations given to the Plural body of the human soul, Adam, who is to be responsible for society. "Who would do such a thing?" Only the few victims of the mindset called Satan, the enemy of all Mankind.

The threat from within from the devolving selfish-interest and arrogance as a motivation within every individual, nation, tribe, and people of man as Mind. Satan, the archetypal enemy of the universal soul, Adam (as) the spiritually regressed, ageless, never-grown-up, teenage rebel in the heavenly garden. The construction of the rationally exaggerated lies of racism, sexism and other Macro-Aggressions are examples of the many, ongoing, rebellious schemes designed to undermine the evolution of the shared soul Adam, male and female. Aoouthu Billahi hir Rahman nir Rahim, and we seek refuge with Allah (swt) from Satan, the rejected enemy within.

Chapter Twelve

The Tree as a Sign for Evolving the Goodly Spirit & Intelligent Life

"Seest thou not how Allah sets forth a parable? A goodly word like a goodly tree, whose root is firmly fixed, and its branches (reach) to the heavens, of its Lord. So, Allah sets forth parables for men, in order that they may receive admonition." Al Qur'an, Yusuf Ali, S. 14, A. 24.

Every human soul has a spiritual, rational, and material urge that must be kept whole to evolve the wholeness and integrity of Man as a Plural Body of humanity responsible for society. What makes culture artificial? Culture becomes artificial to the extent that its socially-constructed language environments mix good and evil influences and deliberately neglect, deconstruct and dissemble guidance, promote exaggerated "rational lies," and uproot or leave out concern for the wholeness of principled logic and universals necessary for the evolution of the shared human soul, Adam, male and female.

One of the root meanings of dead is "insensible, void of perception" or "lacking the sense of something." **Etymonline.com), In that sense, when Man is deliberately cut off from the Spiritual Sciences and uprooted from the Material Sciences, the mind and spirit are dead in terms of lacking the direct perception of the five senses, abilities and faculties that establish Creation-Inspired, Spiritual, Material, Objective, Empirical and Social Sciences.

The visual picture of the Ascension as the evolution of spirit and thinking can be seen as a rooting elevation and evolution of the two elements of the soul as the ability to use reason by the spirit of faith that helps us distinguish right from wrong (Fujuruha wa Taqwaha). Imam Mohammed explains Taqwah as proper regardfulness or G'd consciousness. Taqwah as spirit rising vertically protects Fujur and allows the human being to stand upright in his/her nature. Man as mind grows upright with the support of imagination, intuition and intellect as human faculties that evolve out of the spirit and experience in material creation, like the trunk of a tree that grows upright.

Fujur is understood as a symbolic reference to Fajr, the rising of the sun or dawn in the figurative sense, we speak of conscious awareness *dawning* upon us as reason rising from sincere faith. The Ancient Sphinx facing East toward the rising sun on the plains of Giza is an ancient sign reflecting the logic of Man as mind rising above animal life as ruler of creation with spirit and reason that evolves from creation and the universal soul.

The mental and spiritual faculties, language, and logic of Man as mind, male and female, grow out of the material reality to form a balance of rational and spiritual sensitivity, awareness, intelligence, reason, skill, disciplined authority, freedom self-direction, and control. A discipline of heart and mind as mates (Zawjain) in every human soul, established by keeping the soles/souls of the feet on the ground to support the legs for standing, with arms for balance horizontally like the limbs of a tree.

Artificial Language Environments
Crucify the Body as Symbolic Knowledge

> "Jesus was the Word and Spirit that comes from G'd, and you cannot kill the Spirit that comes from G'd. You cannot crucify it. You cannot kill or crucify the Word that comes from G'd." – Imam Mohammed, Warith Deen (raa). "Moses by Name in the Qur'an More Than Any Other Prophet." Imams Meeting. February 12, 1983. Dallas, TX. Lecture.

> **WORD STUDY**
>
> Media
>
> Related to, Medium, PIE - Medyo
>
> "In the middle, between.
>
> Harper, & Liu, Etymonline.com
>
> Interpretation
> Any socially constructed means of influencing.
>
> a large number of people with the influences of Popular culture.

"The Media Makes Leaders."
IWDM

> *"In concluding this, let me bring to mind another expression in religion that is very common, "son of man." Satan's target is the son of man whom he wants to destroy. If he can't destroy him, at least he wants to make him of no consequence. He wants to crucify him, tie up his forces and arrest his energies and influence if he can't kill him outright Imam Mohammed, W.D., lecture, October 5, 1986, at Masjid Honorable Elijah Muhammad.*

Imam Mohammed's notion that media evolves leadership can be seen in the fact that entertainment, social media and the influences of "street" culture create the stars of entertainment and sports as models for impressionable youth to imitate and identify with as two of the primary means of socialization Imam Mohammed identifies stars with influential people in society and culture. The word influence has in it the sense of something flowing like air or water. Earth or land is firm or fixed and fire flickers as it burns, the faraway stars even the light of the sun flickers and is sometimes totally eclipsed.

Air is a metaphor for socially constructed influences in the environment or what we refer to as the vibe we sense and feel in the social atmosphere. We should reflect on the fact that present day media influences also stream into our mind from the influences and emotional responses that move the shared spirit or ethos of Popular Culture. The social spirit flows like positive and negative influences in the streams of mass media. The flow of water is a symbol for the natural moral influences that flow like rivers, streams, or even atmospheric rivers of weather during seasons of El Nino´ that create destructive storms.

No Fool No Fun!

"Know ye (all), that the life of this world is but play and amusement, pomp and mutual boasting and multiplying, (in rivalry) among yourselves, riches and children. Here is a similitude: How rain and the growth which it brings forth, delight (the hearts of) the tillers; soon it withers; thou wilt see it grow yellow; then it becomes dry and crumbles away. But in the Hereafter is a Penalty severe (for the devotees of wrong). And Forgiveness from Allah and (His) Good Pleasure (for the devotees of Allah). And what is the life of this world, but goods and chattels of deception? Al Qur'an, Yusuf Ali, S. 57., A. 20.

As a process of imitation, identification, reward, and punishment associated with the influences of Popular culture socialization is the first means by which people become people. Popular culture, means for the people especially for impressionable youth. The story of Ham as one destined to serve others because he laughed at his father for example is a story of many continually recycled versions of archetypal influences in culture repeatedly used to create the influences of social scripts to be imitated. Ham is a design promoted in the influences of culture to uproot the heavenly aspirations of the shared soul with social influences that are imitated or rejected by mass publics of common people.

Popular culture is most often designed to be like an artificial tree that represents recycled periods influences of cultural evolution and devolution that promotes the useful abilities of influences on the spirit and thinking and the evolution of society. The lesson of the also mythical story of Ham as a continually recycled myth in the social constructs and influences of Popular culture today is in the old school saying, "no fool no fun." Fool is from "Old French (fol) meaning "to cheat, trick or divert." (Etymonline.com.)

> **WORD STUDY**
>
> **School**
>
> **Greek , "Intermission of work, leisure from work for learning,"**
>
> **Also, School of Hard Knocks = "rough experience in life"**
>
> **Harper, & Liu, Etymonline.com**
>
> **Interpretation**
>
> **Any place and time set aside for study.**
>
> **"School Means Leisure."**
>
> **Etymonline.com**

We should reflect on the word school meaning "leisure." Leisure as the meaning of school refers to the idea that we must take time as the price set aside for study and learning. Meanwhile a life of too much fun or nothing but pleasure-seeking selfish indulgence diverts the soul from the integrity, evolution and development of the human spirit and thinking. The goodly tree represents the logic of culture, which influences the organization and useful abilities of branches of knowledge that inform the spirit and thinking with the bounty of its fruitful ideas, and the beauty of its flowers. The language environments of Traditional Culture and Institutional Culture must produce fruitful ideas, the beauty of flowers, and nectar gathered by busy bees for a cure of honey as signs for those who are mindful. The bounty and beauty of the goodly tree produces a bountiful harvest of fruitful ideas for learning and labor rather than the bankrupting influences of too much fun.

Nuts on a tree are an allusion to the goddess of the sky called Nut in Egyptian mythology. Her Mother is Tefnut, the goddess of rainfall, water, and fertility. And the myths of Egypt are a "tough nut to crack" but Imam Mohammed has given us many of the keys to follow the logic.

Shu (shoe) and nut are twins in Egyptian mythology to the goddess of the sky. Shu, yes, your shoes too, representing the air or social atmosphere are twins too as social constructions protecting your feet. Good shoes protect the feet that establish us in the real world, don't they? Air is also a reference to the social atmosphere that we breathe in or inhale as an allusion to the necessity of breathing that brings us alive and keeps us alive. Inspire means to come alive mentally by breathing in the healthy spirit of a social atmosphere. Social influences bring us alive by continually inspiring our spirit to feel and think. The misspent party life provides an atmosphere of self-indulgent freedom that stifles thinking and reason and diverts the fool to a dead end.

The socially prescribed influences that promote Ham as a type of the deconstructed human soul, being cursed to serve and entertain others aims to maintain the life of spirit and emotion in culture through entertainment and sports. The story of Ham being cursed to live life by entertaining others and self-indulgent party life is associated with us, leaderless, so called "Black" folks, but today is wakeup time! So, "free your mind and free the people'! (J. Tucker, friend).

"Gog" (Head) & "Magog" (No Head)
IWDM

> What is the sun of the solar system? It's the boss, the head, the leader, the ruler, the nucleus for the government that we call the solar system. He wants to destroy the son of man in you. He wants to rob you of your rightful possessions, the government of the individual." — Imam Mohammed, Warith Deen (raa). "Gog and Magog," Muslim Journal, October 31, 1986.

The cultural influences of a lifestyle filled only with nightlife and fun divert the spirit and thinking from the benefit of the scientific and cultural influences of productive life. A nightlife of fun makes for artificial spirits and minds cultivated by the influences of living life in socially constructed artificial darkness. When the artificial language and logic of culture is cut off from the influences of the light of revelation from the heavens (An Nur), the inspiration and motivation of the light of the material creation (As Shams) spirit and thinking become artificial. When our feet are uprooted from establishment as the measure and rule of things in natural reality for material growth, the spirit and thinking become artificial. In the sense that the spirit and word of fun life influences in Popular culture may be misused to "divert, trick, recycle and "curse" the mind with influences that make the mind like the type of mythical Ham as a falsified type of the human soul.

The story of Ham and other artificial social constructs of both good, socially-constructed evil and rational exaggerations and influences are created and disguised as just for fun. Influences that emphasize fun life in culture and language environment divert the innocent soul from its original character, responsibility and destiny.

Social constructions and cultural narratives like the story of Ham with exaggerated influences of fun life uproot the spirit and thinking so the soul as that type is cut off from the light of revelation from heaven above and the inspiration and motivation from the material creation in which the feet are firmly planted. to evolve the soul. An artificial tree of good and evil influences and exaggerated fun life, diverted from the waters of moral life, nutrients from the earth and light for the intelligent life from the heavens is a culture that produces Ham as a cursed type of the soul.

A tree of cultural language and logic that is dead produces an uprooted body of artificial, scientific, and cultural knowledge that also falsifies the influences on human life. A tree of nighttime is the right time fun life without sunlight, to grow leaves for understanding the Material creation. Leaves on a tree produce growth from the sunlight, like the leaves of books preserve knowledge that enlightens and establishes the productive life and abilities (Able) of the shared soul. In a case where the light has gone out of the culture, the original soul can only be resurrected by the light of Revelation, from the Creator of the heavens and the earth.

The growth of spiritual and rational potential is stunted by fun life like a tree; understood as the logic of artificial cultural influences that lack the fresh air of oxygen produced by the leaves. The leaves take out the toxins of carbon dioxide, and produce oxygen and carbohydrates to sustain the life of the tree. The leaves also produce glucose through photosynthesis that requires the daylight of the sun, without which the leaves are left in the darkness of nightlife, like the human intellect. The soul, deprived of clean, fresh air and the light to enlighten the mind with mother nature's language and logic, suffocates in the bad breath and toxic cultural influences of fun life. Thus, the human soul, deprived of light and air by the artificial environment of nightlife, is cut-off from the light of day, and from the spirit which motivates thinking and reason that enlightens the mind for a productive life.

Thus, living the nightlife full of nothing but fun "diverts" the spirit and thinking from the productive life and industry of the original thinker

Adam, male and female. A socially-constructed language environment and uprooted body of scientific and cultural life filled with nothing but fun for fools is dead as support for evolving the productive life for the human soul.

> **WORD STUDY**
>
> Progress
>
> *Pro* = "forward + *gress* (from French, (gradi) = to walk"
>
> Harper, & Liu, Etymonline.com
>
> Interpretation
>
> Progress = to walk or go forward in any way.

Progress Requires Leadership

"Gog and Magog.' Juj-wa-majuj are not original Arabic terms. So, we have to be aware of the meaning of juj and majuj, in the environment where these terms originated. `Juj means, having a head, and `ma-juj' means having no head. It means leaders having leadership, and `ma-juj,' having no leadership. Imam W. Deen Mohammed, 02/26/2002, Muslim Journal, "Savior Day", Charleston, S.C.

"Satan told G'd: 'I am going to go out before them and behind them. I am going to go on their left and on their right.' He was saying to G'd: 'I am going to crucify the whole of Mankind.' And what is crucifying? It is blocking, stopping, checking, making static and still what should be moving for G'd.

The root of the word progress gives the picture of walking or moving forward in any way, in any direction with the power and direction of the intellect and guidance for the spirit and the mind. The bottoms of the feet that allow us to stand up and walk are the soles or metaphoric souls. A symbolic connection with the powers of the potential of the soul and the ability of the legs to stand in prayer (Qiyam) and progress (as Rajilun) the mind and spirit for supporting progress on every path of our Lord. The arms are symbolic of power or strength, and the hands, with thumb and four fingers, are symbolic of control of the power and strength directed by the spirit and mind.

Whatever is useful on any path of progress for establishing every concern by the Will of the Lord of Creation requires that the mind and spirit give direction to make use of the hands that we create with and control our actions with. Man's feet are not rooted in the earth like a tree, but the spirit and mind must be rooted in the language and logic of the creation to give support to the legs to stand up and give guidance that directs the feet. Unlike any animal, Man's head, male and female, is set on top to rule his/her upright body so the two feet and legs can take us in any direction to establish the shared human soul. To have peace in the world, the soul understood as every son/sun, child of Adam, as Mankind, male and female must be established in creation as a ruler of their own soul.

The Mentally & Spiritually Dead

"The cross is a symbol of great advancement, the original state that Allah made the soul to be in, but it is also a symbol of great advancement in the world; that you have achieved balance. Now the ancients also designed the scale that you weigh things in to be a likeness or a symbol for the natural balance that should be in human beings." — Imam Mohammed, Warith Deen (raa). Ramadan Session, 2006. Lecture.

In visualizing the two dimensions of the growth of the spirit and thinking for collective human establishment as a symbolic representation of the Plural Body of Man "who must be responsible for society," the Sirat al Mustaqim, represents vertical movement. The Sirat represents evolution of the soul with spiritual balance on two feet, with heart as the center and the head on top. As Sabil, the way seeker, represents rational or horizontal growth, and the balance of arms outstretched from the body horizontally are like the branches of a tree. The growth of the tree depends on water and minerals from the roots deep in the earth (Al Ard) below and the light of the sun from the heavens (As Samaa) above.

> *"So, this Seraat is really a path of knowledge, it is more than that, but its strongest reference is to the path of knowledge, the path of the development of your brain, your human intellect. This is the path for the development of the human as a rational being with an intellect, so it is Seraat Al Mustaqeem."* Imam Mohammed, WD, 10-7-2007 Ramadan Sunday Session, Homewood, Ill.

The growth of Man as mind begins with direct experience and engagement with the material reality that feeds the spirit and mind. The roots grow deep in the soil to keep the tree planted upright. Rather than being planted in the soil, Man stays rooted in material creation by using the potentials of common sense, imagination, thinking, intuition, and reason. The primal cultures of the first men as mind develop from direct experience in the natural world. Faculties and abilities that develop the awareness of feeling, thinking and reason rule the head with the hard-earned lessons of study experience and education from the material creation.

The tree and other plant life are signs for the growth and development of culture in the natural world. The tree grows vertically from the earth and spreads its limbs and branches from its trunk, which is rooted deep in the material logic of the sciences of creation in the earth. Man stands up in his human nature and rationally balances on two feet understood as measures inherent in the soul/soles. The trunk of the human body is supported by the legs and feet. The right foot and leg symbolize Fujur, the Fajr of standing up as the dawning of intellect, and the left foot/leg symbolizes ese se volution of common sense as rooted in Taqwah, inborn and innate spiritual sensitivities of G'd-consciousness created in the soul.

As inherent potentials of every human soul, common sense and reason evolve to support the legs of intelligent life that depend on the abilities of fujur as conscious awareness and reason that enable us to make progress as going forward in every way. Animals are bound to the earth on all fours by the physical urges, animal instincts and senses of the animal are limited to reacting to the influences of the natural environment that dictates animal behavior.

The trunk of the body has organs in all three sections: 1. the reproductive organs below the waist, 2. the abdomen above the waist ruled by urges and appetites, and 3. the chest heart and lungs above the diaphragm. Unlike the trunk of the tree these are the vital organs that sustain life and support the conscious and unconscious life, Organs are vital inputs for the head that exercises authority and discipline over the urges of reproduction, the appetites of the gut and the heart, if not you may lose your mind. The heart is the companion or mate (Zawj) of the mind. (Imam Salahuddin Hanif)

The spirit and thinking allow us to balance upon the sensitive feet, when kept planted firmly on the ground. The feet are symbolic of establishment in creation-inspired language and logic that evolve from the Material Sciences. Logic from material creation informs development, mastery of the individual and collective self as a Plural Body of community life for evolving the ideas and influences of culture and direction for civilized progress.

Rationally-constructed exaggerations and lies in the Spiritual, Material and Social Sciences are a means of creating the mentally and spiritually dead. A sleep or death of the conscience, conscious awareness, social sentiments, intellect, thinking, and reason, to support social establishment, culture, and community life. If the body as knowledge is uprooted and falls down into the socially constructed influence of the mentally and spiritually dead the soul, created by G'd may go to sleep or die.

For the believer guided by Al Qur'an as Source and the Prophet's example (saw), the result is direction for the enlightened mind and soul for evolving a wholistic body of knowledge. An informed individual and Plural Body of community life are moved first and last to think with the spirit of rational faith like Abraham the Father of Faith. An Al Qur'an as Source, Ascension-Based, Creation-Inspired model removes the foundation of philosophical theory and book knowledge upon which the Objective Sciences are based. Book learning alone creates an artificial floor and ceiling to education in creation. Studying the foundations of the uprooted theories, philosophies, and sciences of socially-constructed, artificial language and logic can only make us somebody else's book worms. Freedom and responsibility for the wholistically-informed human intellect is a necessity for complete establishment of Man "who must be responsible for society" (Mohammed). Allah has created nothing higher than the intellect, (Aql.)

Let us follow the logic like direct orders as wisdom from Imam Mohammed given to us in 1982, and "throw out all of their books" until we have established our own perception of the heavens, the earth and Man's establishment and evolution as a universal soul! We need not accept anyone else's vision of Scriptural Reasoning as a spiritual and intellectual and artificial floor or "glass ceiling" from the East or West that seals off the growth of both light of Creation in every sign and truth (Ayah and Haqq) in every book of creation and revelation was sent down from the heavens by the Lord of all the systems of Knowledge.

Division in the Social & Material Sciences Creates Division in the Soul & Psyché

Chapter (90) Sūrat l-Balad (The City)

> 8. "Have We not made for him a pair of eyes?- 9. And a tongue, and a pair of lips?- 10. And shown him the two highways? 11. But he hath made no haste on the path that is steep. Yusuf Ali, S. 90, A. 8-11.

Division in the potentials of the universal human soul or Psyché is created by artificial divisions of the social, material, and spiritual influences and the understanding and application of the Sciences that produce language environments and culture. Thus, as common people we may lack the capability to achieve a balance in the individual, social, rational, and material struggle of everyday life and civilized human interest. The separation, juxtaposition and division of the spirit and thinking (the elements of the soul) are seen in the exaggerated emphasis on the Cain Principle, the extreme pursuit of material progress, Material Sciences, material logic, material power, domination and influence as more essential than spiritual, rational and social concerns that support and guide the complete progress of civilized life.

In most cultures, the public masses of common people often have little or no access to education in the principled logic, universals of academics and higher education reserved for privileged elites. Elites are selected, supported, informed, empowered, and elevated in social hierarchies of power, money, influence, and knowledge as power by academic language and "dry" logic or cryptic language and logic used to rule the common masses.

As the managers of institutions, elites, especially those who are elected as social servants and political leaders and town fathers, should be sworn as servants of social life and culture rather than devolving into the beneficiaries of personal wealth, power, and privilege.

The mass publics of common humanity whose spirit and thinking are trained for work primarily in the use of practical skills and application of muscle power and the logic and language required for hard labor and basic skills.

The prescription for the shared soul as a Plural Body of model community life is to be dedicated to supporting the public masses with the vision and tools that promote spiritual and rational development of the common soul. Al Qur'an as source for logic, language and construction of culture provides definition and direction for building every house for every human concern represented by the design of the house of Mecca built by Abraham (as) for the benefit of all Mankind.

The Spirit & Word Evolve from the Soul.
Chapter (3) Sūrat āl 'Im'rān (The Family of Imrān)

"The similitude of Jesus before Allah is as that of Adam; He created him from dust, then said to him: 'Be.' And he was." Al Qur'an, Yusuf Ali, S. 3, A. 59.

Metaphoric language from misconstrued stories of scripture speak to how the human soul is crucified and resurrected as Man meaning mind, male and female. As Jesus said of himself in relation to every human soul, "I in you and you in me," meaning the spirit and word in the human soul created by G'd is a potential in every human soul!

African-Americans were enslaved by predatory materialists as an experimental plan for the enslavement and subjugation of the universal human soul of all of Mankind! A rational lie from a false interpretation of scripture that cursed African-Americans to become the enslaved servants of others.

What happened to the human souls of enslaved Africans during and after the middle passage? Enslaved peoples were stripped of all the language and logic of culture and civilized life that forms the mind and spirit. Corrupt influences used in the service of deconstruction reduce the human soul to the level of animal life. The most sophisticated, deliberate, complete domination and oppression in history, attempting to make the human soul, the slave of men. Falsifying the human soul of slaves with the curse of Ham, the son of Noah and slavery as the Will of G'd that created the system of chattel slavery that cursed both slave and master.

What happened to enslaved Africans was founded on an archetypal plan that began with Adam and the schemes of the enemy of mankind, in the heavenly garden within Man. Satan, understood as an influence in every Man as mind, male and female that devolves into selfish interest, open opposition and a will to dominate the universally-shared soul.

Corrupt Means to Break the Heart

Corrupt means to break the heart. Language environments that corrupt the heart, mind and behavior break the spiritual, moral, and emotional sensitivities of the heart. This implies that a corrupt use of the principle of Social Science called Environmental Determinism is a product of both the natural and social environment.

The word cryptic means hidden or concealed, and a crypt is a place to bury the dead, usually in the earth. So, connecting these terms we can say a crypt is a socially-constructed language environment in which to bury the original human soul, Adam, and the second Ascension level, Jesus, son of Mary, the types of every human soul. A socially-constructed cryptic burial of the spirit and word of creation in the material logic of socially-constructed rational lies kills or puts the human spirit to sleep by attempting to crucify the word that forms the naturally innocent human spirit and mind.

That is why in the Qur'an, it says: 'No, neither did they kill him, nor did they make him static and still. They did not give him rigor mortis.' This fourth phase of righteous deeds will take us all down off the cross. Taqwah, by itself, cannot take us off the cross. The cross is static life, where you can't move." — Imam Mohammed, Warith Deen (raa). "By the Token of Time, By the Hour." April 12, 2002, Salatul Jumu'ah Khutbah at the Atlanta Masjid of Al-Islam. Atlanta, GA.

Human beings become conditioned to be kept in their place by social barriers, name-calling, and the spirit of inferiority when cryptic language, or hidden principles of artificial language and logic. Macro - and Micro-Aggressions represented as rationally-constructed language and logic, capture the emotions and imagination with socially-constructed confusion. Language that deconstructs, "Nijjerizes " or reduces human nature to the socially constructed status of being dependent like boys and girls or animals whose lives must be managed. The seeds for deconstruction of human sensitivities are also rooted in the living conditions of social environments like slave quarters and segregated ghettoes. And language environments in media influences that create popular culture habits and attitudes like the drug culture and gangster life in many social environments.

Much like the blood sports of the Roman gladiators, the spirit of the common people is influenced by entertainment like that of the circus of Ancient Rome. Modern day strategies are similarly used for holding the social sentiments, imagination, common sense, the spirit, and aspirations of mass publics in check while neglecting the need for the principled logic of universal education.

The spirit and mind can be influenced by every sort of artificially-constructed, problem that plays on the ignorance of the physical, social, and cultural corruption in language environments. Thus, still today artificial language and logic are used to keep life static for those deemed as less than other human beings often living in the hood. Cryptic or coded language, socially-constructed influences and academic, "dry" logic create ignorance and corrupt influences that dehumanize and strip away the human potential and abilities, leaving the soul dependent upon socially-constructed, cultural environments.

Many original and traditional "soul" people and others in and outside of the "hoods" still are not able to construct or control their language environments, social systems, or cultural life. Others are awakening to the artificial, cultural influences that kill independent leadership for the spirit and thinking in the plural body, especially Muslim African-Americans. Adam is the first potential of every soul as spirit and mind created to tell all the angels their names. And it is way past wake-up time!

Satan Lies in Wait in Language Environments
Chapter (7) Sūrat l-A'rāf (The Heights)

He said: "Because thou hast thrown me out of the way, lo! I will lie in wait for them on thy straight way. Al Qur'an, Yusuf Ali, S. 7, A. 16.

As noted in the commentary of Imam Warith Deen Mohammed (raa) on language construction, "As we don't know that Al Qur'an reveals to us the most important construction is not the material construction, it is the linguistic or language construction. It says, 'He laid the foundation of the House,' it is talking about the Ka'bah."

Shaytan's vow *la-aq'udanna*, "surely I will lie in wait," is related to the same word for language environments, grammar, and foundation *Al Qawā'id* اَلْقَوَاعِدَ , meaning sitting position, foundation, and grammar or language environment. Al Qawā'id is also used in Al Baqarah (The Cow) S. 2, A.127.

"And remember Abraham and Isma'il raised the <u>foundations</u> (اَلْقَوَاعِدَ) of the House (With this prayer): "Our Lord! Accept (this service) from us: For Thou art the All-Hearing, the All-knowing." Al Qur'an, Yusuf Ali, S. 2, A. 127.

Al Qawā'id can also mean principles, rules, or models. Similarly, Jalasa means to sit, and Majlis means social gathering. These words demonstrate that shared language and logic begin the social process to evolve the principled life, language and logic of community life and establish the vision for the institutions of civilized life.

The Cross:
"A Sign of the Original State that (G'd) Allah Made the Soul to Be In." IWDM

> *"You heard the expression 'double cross?' That is what Satan did to us. Allah made our nature to be in the right balance. The Prophet, peace be upon him, said, 'Qul amantu fastaqim.' Say, 'I have believed and thereafter be upright'. So, the balance that G-d created in our nature for us is upright, and actually every human being evolves to stand up erect.*
>
> *And all you have to do is raise your arms on a level with your shoulders and you form a cross. So, the cross also is a sign of the uprightness, the balance that Allah created us for. And obviously Satan, Shaytan, wanted to deprive Man of that balance in his nature. It was lost when he refused G-d's plan for human beings because Satan was cast down and told to do what? 'Bite the dust. Crawl on your belly.' That's where your problem is in your stomach. So, what you're going after is going to pull you down upon your stomach, and you are going to have to crawl on your stomach. Your stomach will be your legs."* — Imam Mohammed, Warith Deen (raa). Ramadan Session. 2006. Lecture.

The tree represents culture, and wood cut from the tree and arranged as a cross is an esoteric symbol with hidden meanings as an artificial tree of culture and social influences. It is an artificial tree of good and evil in symbolic or figurative language and cryptic logic presented as an allegory story or theoretical logic designed to uproot the mind from creation and the crucify the soul.

The symbolic idea of taking the soles of the feet off the ground of material reality implies cutting off human potential from original nature that evolves from Fitratu-llahi of material creation. One sense of the word crucify is to subdue, mortify or torture, implying to put to death by fixing or "nailing" the spirit and word of the body, the sign of useful and ethical knowledge, to the narratives of an artificial language environment, the symbolic tree.

This hanging of the body with the feet off the ground makes the spirit and potential for experience and common-sense dead to the original nature of the creation and the reality of Man's own nature. Thereby, rendering the universally-shared potential created by G'd Almighty incapable of using its original potential of the common soul.

The allegorical, theoretical, and metaphysical story of crucifixion in picture language depicts a symbolic design of an artificial language and logic design for crucifying with artificial culture. A socially-constructed artificial language environment that can be used in the attempt to kill the natural life, innocent spirit of the soul and shared human potential of a Plural Body of people, oppressors and the oppressed included!

When the spirit and mind are uprooted from the logic of creation the arms and hands become powerless, and control over the body for self-direction is lost. When the limbs of the body are spread and the feet and hands are "nailed" to artificial logic, freedom for the original nature of the soul to evolve is lost.

Language Environments Provide the Breath of Life

Chapter (32) Sūrat l-Sajdah (The *Prostration*)

"But He fashioned him in due proportion and breathed into him something of His spirit. And He gave you (the faculties of) hearing and sight and feeling (and understanding): little thanks do ye give!" Al Qur'an, Yusuf Ali, S.32, A.5.

> **WORD STUDY**
>
> Logos/Logic
>
> The Greek "*logos* means the Divine word."
>
> Related: Logic, "leg, to pick out choose" as with the intellect
>
> Harper, & Liu, Etymonline.com
>
> Interpretation
>
> The ability to pick out or choose the best of Man's logic, universals of reason, and judgment based on the divine word.

In the metaphoric sense of crucifixion of the body as a sign representing knowledge the body is hung up in the air and the feet nailed with the exactness of the artificial logic of culture. Being "hung up in the air," is symbolic of being influenced to breathe in (inspiration) the words and artificial social influences, from the atmosphere of a corrupt logic and language environment of artificial culture. The natural life of the original spirit (Ruh) and words that make Man can be deprived of an atmosphere to breath (as in inhale and inspire) by the logic of an artificial language environment that cannot support the natural life of the original soul. Artificial influences that are breathed in from the artificial atmosphere of a language environment can keep the spirit and mind occupied with ideas and influences that block, stop, check, and make static and still "what should be moving for G'd." The key to this idea of breath in mythology is implied in the myth of Shu, the g'd of the air in Egyptian mythology.

Keep Your Feet on the Ground & Your Head to the Sky!
Chapter (6) Sūrat l-An'ām (The Cattle)

> "And when he saw the sun rising, he cried: 'This is my Lord! This is greater!' But when the sun set, he said, 'O my people!

Surely, I am free from that which you associate with God.'"
"For me, I have set my face, firmly and truly, towards Him Who created the heavens and the earth, and never shall I give partners to Allah." Al Quran, Yusuf Ali, S. 6, A. 78-79.

G'd's Promise to Abraham in Genesis

"Then He brought him outside and said, 'Look now toward heaven, and count the stars if you are able to number them.' And He said to him, 'So shall your descendants be.'" (NKJV Bible, Genesis. 15.15.)

The uprooted tree is a symbol of how scientific, social, and cultural knowledge of the sciences of creation can be made artificial. When the artificial language, logic and atmosphere of culture are cut off from the light of heaven from above, the inspiration and motivation from connection to Mother Nature and the material creation directly beneath our feet, the spirit and word of G'd will slip, die or go to sleep in Man understood as the nature of the spirit and mind, Adam, male and female.

Artificial language environments attempt to cut off the spirit and word of creation from nourishment below and the light for the spirit and mind from the heavens above. Artificial language environments influence us to leave the spirit and guidance of revelation for establishing thinking, reason and the rational faith of Abraham (as) the Father of Faith for Muslims, Christians, and Jews. Such an artificial language environment creates a body of uprooted, crucified, artificial culture designed to bury the spirit and mind in artificial logic constructs until the natural life is Zombified or dead.

What would be the result of leaving the mind without a foundation for social and material establishment? A ghostly, spook life of artificial, socially-constructed, artificial material life and institutional establishment based on an artificially-constructed spirit and mind. An immature and devolving mind and spirit blessed to be allowed to sit by the door as dependents of privileged elites, autocrats and oligarchs who rule civilized life from the Big House as the Masters of artificial culture.

When we keep our feet on the ground and our heads to the sky, for G'd-given common sense to evolve our whole hearts and minds we receive more of the guidance of G'd, guidance from the heavens like Father Abraham (as). Thus, we evolve naturally upon both our naturally sensitive human spirit and common-sense faculties rather than being "caught up" in the socially-constructed atmosphere of artificial language environments.

Without the soles of both feet on the ground, we have neither the power to control our spirit nor the word that evolves from the original nature and common sense that informs the intelligent life, reason and the wisdom that evolves from real experience. An uprooted, artificial tree of cultural logic and language results in losing the ability to establish the shared reality of culture, social logic, and language environment.

An artificial tree of socially constructed good and evil without the light of reason results in an environment of rational influences and spiritual darkness. When the light of creation and revelation are cut-off, from the soul, the spirit and mind are crucified, and the spirit and light for "Remaking the World' of civilized life will be lost!

Poem

Goodness Rising

I - am - spirit, of every sun-drenched soul, canonized by the challenge,
of three million years. Tinted by mother earth,
in genteel hues,
Dressed to toil, afar off land....
Groomed, with judicious skill.
Peering from firstborn, heart and mind....
Set...on the journey, By the Mighty G'd, of oneness and time....

Africa gave my being and infinite yearning a tan,
Harsh Europa, schooled my wit, straightened my hair, bleaching my skin.
Guiding the step from deep in the soul....
Building - where mighty temples crumbled long ago....
Tehuantepec, Ephesus and Thebes, Timbuktu, Zimbabwe, Katmandu,
    Mandalay....
Rivers of rain, cleansing the ruin, rising... in sun dried mists,
    enlivened again and again.

Two hundred and fifty centuries ago
I crossed Beringia, in woolly mammoth clothes, spreading to the end
    of a new earth....... Closing the circle, from east and west...with
    a greeting on the unknown shore,
Of turkey, maize, time-honored culture - and pyramid lore

Driven to the market, displayed as threadbare goods......Forging the
    tool, pulling the plow, picking the field.... bearing the market's
    load! ...Fishing the sea, laying lengthy track, making the needy
    prayer.... Marching to war ... along the parched road....

Debased in Sambo darkness…Bleached, and colored with wasted paint,
Emancipated, in a multi-colored sacrament of, red, white and blue ……
Alexander made the short cut - employing his sharpened sword….

Every enslavement has tested, but cannot replace my virtue; Hate used me,
yet left me unspoiled. Oppression touched me - yet I am tenderly
      clean.
Vanity and arrogance possessed me, then left me repentant, for mercy
      to claim…
Guilt and shame have seized me, again and again.
Yet faultless as Adam, on primeval ground
I stand….
Each profitless foe - lain eternally low…lain
Low together, for mercy…. to claim

Fashioning the word, guiding the sturdy hand, every enslavement
      attacking my will.
Still - I - build, where mighty wonders fell…. Tenochtitlan, Khanbaliq,
      Kushiya, and Rhodes…. Prudence erecting the bulwark, again
      and again….

Every, G-d-given, sun drenched soul,
Planted - like Adam - in primeval soil,
Pristine promise - soaring on wings,
Enduring wisdom - judicious skill,
Claimed by mercy……again and again….
Redeemed - in gut - and heart - and mind….
Set - on the journey, by the Mighty G-d,
Of Oneness………and time…

HAE © 2-1-97

PART FIVE

Remaking The World of Academics with Universal Concepts & Scriptural Reasoning.

Chapter Thirteen

Remaking the World of Academic & Material Sciences

"Four Days Measure Supplied all Things" – IWDM

"And the spirit for Man's purpose in life is represented for the human interest is represented by the number three not four, the society, the environment, is represented by four and the environmental potential in Man. You see, Man is a product of the environment, too, and the environmental potential in Man is four, and G'd has given every creature or its provision in four measures this is Qur'an 'in four measures.'" — Imam Mohammed, Warith Deen (raa). Imams Retreat III, January 16, 1999, Randolph, VA. Lecture.

"Al Islam is a complete way of life," and the academic sciences establish reason as a support for the spiritual life within Man. Man organizes the ideas that come to represent culture from the natural influences of creation that support human nature, aspirations, and respect for the universal human destiny. Those universals are expressed in the measure of fours as the Unity of Universals in Creation

---

"Out of the four bases come other fours, still under the material concept. But you have academics, you have political science, you have all of these sciences coming out of that: the four essential sciences that Man needs in order to live and make progress on

this earth." — Imam Mohammed, Warith Deen (raa). "Symbolic Language." *Imam Warith Deen Mohammed Speaks From Harlem, N.Y. 1984*, Harlem, NY. Lecture.

As a means of establishing Man's evolution in civilized life, universal influences in culture support the development of both spirit and thinking as requirements for living a complete human life. There are three sciences required to evolve, support, guide and govern human nature:

"The Sciences"
IWDM

1. Spiritual Sciences,
2. Social Sciences,
3. Material and Objective Sciences.

Four rivers, four birds and four mountains begin as urges in the human soul.

There are four domains of human need, knowledge and established life required to establish institutions, and the unity of universals in civilized life.

1. Education, and the Academic Sciences
2. Culture, and Social Sciences:
   (a) Primal Culture that evolves from the natural environment of creation, and (b.) Traditional Culture, that evolves with social interactions (c.) Institutional Culture, that evolves with Academic Sciences and (d.) Popular Culture, or "Street" culture that is established for people with the influences of media, entertainment, politics and Government.
3. The Science of Economics that evolves with Industry and Business.
4. Political Science. that evolves with Government.

The evolution of these sciences as domains of knowledge and established life begins with the spirit of common sense promoted by socialization that begins in the spirit of family, as the basic unit of society. Common sense that evolves with formal education that supports thinking and reason, for practical and ethical use of the universals of language, and logic. The basis of respect for cultures in establishing themselves and remaining viable is founded on universals that respect the common human soul, Adam, male and female, as in respect for the sacred ideal implied by, "All Men are Created Equal."

Cultural Insanity: The Socially-Constructed, Recycled Influences of Culture Wars

Our adapted definition of "Cultural Insanity" follows from the concept originated by Jeffrey Wynter Koon as influences "that thwart human development." Our further adaptation asserts that Cultural Insanity is 1. the result of any socially-constructed dissembling or deconstruction that undermines socialization, education, and shared awareness, as support for the original nature of every human soul. And 2. promoting cultural influences that deconstruct the natural disposition, spiritual and rational principles of material creation and human nature. (Fitrah & Fitratullahi). Cultural Insanity exists at every level of social hierarchy because of the influences of the regressive mentality of antisocial, selfish-interest, predatory sentiment, and pursuit of absolute domination over other human souls.

Cultural Insanity, Socially-Constructed Influences, & Clinical Symptoms

Chapter (38) Sūrat Sād

75. "(Allah) said: 'O Iblis! What prevents thee from prostrating thyself to one whom I have created with my hands? Art, thou haughty? Or art thou one of the high (and mighty) ones?'"

76. "(Iblis) said: 'I am better than (from) him: thou createdst me from fire, and him thou createdst from clay.'" Al Qur'an, Yusuf Ali, S. 38 A. 75-76.

The understanding and description of individual clinical symptoms, diagnostic criteria, and the symptom picture of personal or individual insanity are similarly reflected in Cultural Insanity. This "better from him" rather than "better than him," as translated and explained by Imam Qasim Ahmed (raa), is a profound Qur'anic insight into the beginning of the problem as a rebellious potential of every human soul. A spirit and mentality that seeks to dominate and control every influence on civilized life through self-serving power, scientifically-exaggerated philosophical or socially-constructed ideological influences in social life and culture. We call that mindset Shaitan, the oldest-but-never-grown-up, teen rebel in the Garden, and we seek refuge from Shaitan in our own selves!

Racism and Sexism
As Classic Cases of Macro-Aggression
Chapter (2) Sūrat Al Baqarah

"And behold We said to the angels: 'Bow down to Adam;' and they bowed down not so Iblis he refused and was haughty he was of those who reject Faith." Al Qur'an, Yusuf Ali, S.2, A. 34.

Macro-Aggressions are rationally-constructed ideas, language constructs and influences of corrupt logic and language environments that deconstruct and falsify the meaning, value and identity of the shared, human soul understood as Adam, male and female. The terms Microaggression and Maco-Aggressions were coined by Harvard psychiatrist Chester Pierce in 1970. (Wikipedia.org)

As socially-constructed language environments and cultural influences, racism, sexism and other Macro-Aggressions, foster alienation and anomie that undermine social norms and the institutions of culture by creating social conflict, normlessness, and disrespect for the moral sentiments that uphold civility and social convention. The result is the breakdown of shared values, rules, civility, reason, mutual respect, and moral, ethical, and legal barriers. Alienation between the ingroup, outgroup or the powerful and dependent among socially constructed outcasts creates the influences of Cultural Insanity. Those who suffer the symptomatic effects of the social sentiments and behavior include the privileged and powerful as well as those deemed to be the aberrant, uncivilized, alien "other." or lower than animals. The socially constructed result? A socially constructed environment of Cultural Insanity and devolution of civilized life.!

The ambivalent alternation of construction and deconstruction of human nature, dissembling of language environments and the shared human identity of Adam (as) occurs in the influences and shared, social sentiments of virtually every society. Macro-Aggressions are the biggest influences impeding the struggle for universal freedom for every human soul. Racism and sexism are the classic examples of socially constructed Macro-Aggressions and devolution of human nature as a shared soul in the Modern World. Macro-Aggressions create an unnatural ambivalence motivated by a predatory, self-interested mentality as a disposition that manifests in the pathos ethos and suffering of the shared human soul in every oppressive, socially constructed language environment. Conflicts in social life and culture are expressed in the oppression and subjugation of both the powerful and the many by the socially-constructed influences of Macro-Aggressions. Any spirit that undermines universal respect for mutual rights under the law and allows for the deconstruction of the institutions of society and civilized life qualifies as a Macro-Aggression.

Slaves as Three fifths of a Man, A Socially Constructed Macro-Aggression!

There are many examples of Macro-aggressions as social policy and law such as the Missouri compromise, and the Dred Scott decision, which denied slaves as being citizens. In spite of the considerable effort to prohibit slavery under the constitution. And the compromise making slaves 3/5th of a man. Much of human history in every civilization has diminished the human potential of others by erecting legal barriers and language constructions and environments to create Macro-Aggressions.

"A Sacred Rule" Of Socially Constructed Hierarchies

The obligation of human beings to create culture and language environments implies that the reality of social life and culture can be entirely a result of narratives (stories) created by men who are assumed to be transcendent masters of an otherwise g'd-less universe. The word environment and social scripts of culture are constructed by men who may or may not respect the sacred obligation of the sciences, academics and philosophical influences being and their ethical use, supported by the revealed word of scripture. Thus, we may have a hierarchy or sacred rule over a universe left to men by an "absent g'd," with no ethical obligation to respect the spiritual, rational, or social, universals from which every human soul evolves.

Self-interested motives in such a world all but inevitably misleads some to seek power and domination over all others in the sense of "I am better from him." The attitude expressed as the rebellion of one of the Jinn against the plan for Adam. Almighty G-d has deemed the enemy of Mankind as a potential also within every human soul!

Macro-Aggressions & Micro-Aggressions, Cultural Insanity & Communal Trauma in Language Environments

> "It irks Satan that Man takes this responsibility on himself and keeps Satan out of it. So, he says: 'How can they keep me out of something I was in before they were in it? I used to lead the

Angels. I am going to outthink them and crucify the whole race of Mankind.'

Satan told G'd: 'I am going to go out before them and behind them. I am going to go on their left and on their right.' He was saying to G'd: 'I am going to crucify the whole of Mankind.' And what is crucifying? It is blocking, stopping, checking, making static and still what should be moving for G'd." — Imam Mohammed, Warith Deen (raa). "By the Token of Time, By the Hour..." Salatul Jumu'ah Khutbah at the Atlanta Masjid of Al-Islam, April 12, 2002. Atlanta, GA.

Socially-constructed, Macro-Aggressive influences and ideas undermine shared human sentiments, thinking, reason and the universal perception of human nature as a shared soul. Cultural and ideological Macro-Aggressions such as racism, sexism and other exaggerated, ideological, and philosophical extremes induce trauma in culture, social and individual life. The influences of racial or ethnic supremacy, tribal, nationalistic, or other self-serving artificial ideas create abnormal social and cultural conflicts and communal trauma.

There are two main dimensions of the spectrum of artificially-constructed influences and ideas that induce Cultural Insanity and communal trauma that manifest as, social sentiments and clinical symptoms:

1. Socially constructed Anomie: A breakdown in social sentiments that results in the deconstruction of ethical norms and standards in mutually-disaffected communities and groups.
2. Socially Constructed Alienation: influences in language constructions that separate and isolate communities, ethnic groups, as shared or individual identities based on falsification of human nature.
3. The concept of Cultural Insanity may be extended to include any concept, socially constructed language and logic that promotes incivility, and anti-social sentiments toward any human soul, son of

Adam as separate and apart from the identity of Man as mind, male and female.

The term *clinical* implies a focus on care for the individual patient, but socially-constructed, artificial language environments induce symptomatic expressions of Cultural Insanity in the collective consciousness or shared self as a Plural body of humanity. The Plural body of the soul created as One Soul (Nafsin Wahidah), the collective or shared self and collective conscience of which function on the same patterns of logical and ethical principles as the individual self, created as Adam. And Adam is the father expressed in the innate potentials of every soul, male and female of every nation, tribe, and people.

Socially constructed Macro-Aggressions in language environments create anomie alienation and Micro-Aggressions, in individual and communal interactions. The result clinically and symptomatically, is Cultural Insanity, shared personal, communal, emotional, mental, and spiritual trauma in the Plural body of shared souls.

The causal factors of communal trauma begin with the influences, social constructions, and ideological language constructions of Macro-Aggressions. Macro-Aggressions engender interactions that induce symptoms such as detachment of spirit from reason, imagination from thinking, alienation depression, suppression, and division of personal and social interest, diminishing and marginalization of rights, abilities, and freedom, independent thinking, responsibilities. Social and cultural Macro-Aggressions and Micro-Aggressions undermine the civilized urge for establishing shared sentiments, civilized behavior, the universals that support spiritual balance and rational faith as support for conscious life and direction in evolving civilized life.

Healthy social and cultural environments seek to integrate the social and cultural influences that support psychological and social wellness. The extremes of socially-constructed Macro-Aggressions are causal mechanisms that underlie personal and communal trauma, social maladjustment, and mental illness as symptomatic expressions of emotional and mental illness. The socially constructed symptomatic expression of Macro-Aggressions can be defined along every dimension of the spectrum of neuroses and psychoses.

Recycling of Macro-Aggressions & Micro-Aggressions

"You Need a Moment of Peace…"
IWDM

> "Satan knows that if Man can ever be left at peace long enough, he will come into his own. But Satan knows that if he can keep Man in conflict and at war within himself, he will never develop to his potential. You need a moment of peace to get yourself together."
> — Imam Mohammed, Warith Deen (raa). "Savior Day," Muslim Journal. February 26, 2002. Charleston, S.C.

One of the original examples of the construction of influences that engender and continually recycle the symptoms of Cultural Insanity, are the rational exaggerations and language barriers in the Modern World the based on the legal prohibitions of the "slave codes." Slave Codes forbade enslaved people from learning to read or write and punished "Whites" who taught them. A recycled version of the scheme of institutionalizing Macro-Aggressions to undermine thinking and reason such as the varied strategies of Jim Crow segregation that continued to exploit both races long after the emancipation of slaves.

"Break the Yokes of Oppression."
IWDM

Chapter (21) Sūrat l-Anbiyāa (The Prophets)

> "And We have not sent you, [O Muhammad], except as a mercy to the worlds." Al Qur'an, Sahih International S. 21, A. 107.

> "And we witness that Muhammed (pbuh), the Last or the Seal of Prophets, came to break all the bonds of slavery, all forms of slavery, especially moral slavery, and mental slavery, to the world of sin and wickedness. Also, it is said of him, that he would take off the heavy yoke that weighs the people down.
>
> This is speaking to the oppression of human beings by corruption and by the forces of Satan, or as we call him in Islam "Shaitan." Muhammed was born in the city of Mecca in the land of the Arabs, now called Saudi Arabia. Also of him, it says that he is a mercy to all of the worlds and a mercy to all people. He is not just a mercy to one people, but to all the people on earth and to all the worlds and nations." — Imam Mohammed, Warith Deen (raa). "Savior Day," Muslim Journal. February 26, 2002. Charleston, S.C.

Age-old, archetypal attitudes, language, social and cultural constructions, rational exaggerations and falsified "Isms" have been promoted since the creation of Adam, and Allah (swt) the Mighty and Wise Knows Best! The exaggerated use of the coded, often-cryptic language and logic of race, gender, and other artificial "Isms" and their socially-constructed, oppressive uses have been continuously recycled. Macro-Aggressions are the foundation of artificial ideological and philosophically-constructed language environments. Unlike the racism and sexism of the last 400 years, Modern-Day, socially-constructed culture wars are not new, having origins in the disposition and attitude expressed in the statement of the Shaitan in Surah 7, Ayat 12 of Al Qur'an," I am better from Him" (Ana Kairun Minhu.)

Oppression of the sensitive life and social sentiments allows the self-serving enemy of Mankind to control human nature and attempt to uproot, crucify, divide, and devolve the human soul. Socially-constructed, Cultural Insanity is designed to limit the shared spirit, shared perception, common sense, thinking social emotions, communal interests, and moral accountability of Man as Mind.

There are many such, present-day forms of coded language promoted by billion-dollar media enterprises that weaponize "alternative facts" and "fake news" to falsify culture and human perception. The reactionary denial created by Culture wars allows mutual fear and hate to be placed on temporary hold in subconscious denial by disguising and redesigning, even reversing the social narratives and regressive attitudes of Macro-Aggressions. Thus, the logic of Macro-Aggressions is placed in cold-storage in service to the possibility of re-erecting its narratives, social agenda, legal barriers, and social policies that silence criticism and dissent by whitewashing history.

Socially-constructed Cultural Insanity is used in service to domination of shared life by self-serving authority in pursuit of material wealth and power through oppression of the evolving, human soul. Strategies such as the use of "alternative facts" disguise the old language, and falsified meanings of self-confessed, self-serving falsehoods that conceal, redesign, and continually recycle Cultural Insanity. The effect of such divisive influences aims to perpetuate the devolution of social life, culture, and healthy, psychological, and social attitudes. Devolution to the point where falsehoods are openly used as tools in everyday service to maintain the status quo of Cultural Insanity in social life and institutions.

Please Do Not Resuscitate!

Another example of socially-constructed Macro-Aggressions expressed in the disguise, denial, projection and passive-aggressive motives of language constructions is the recycled notion of abolishing Diversity, Equity, and Inclusion (DEI) initiatives. Initiatives designed to address the long-term, measurable effects of racism and its continual influences on culture. An odd kind of denial of real history, through reaction formation, projection and recycling symptomatic, of socially and culturally prescribed policies buoyed upon legal strategies, judgements, and regressive psychological and social assumptions.

Prejudice Is an Attitude, Racism = Prejudice + Power

Is racism still systematic? Yes and No! Prejudice is an attitude; racism is a system of legally sanctioned prejudice plus power! Yes, racism is on its deathbed, prejudice is not! Most of the legal structures of legalized socially sanctioned Racism are being eroded after having been recycled in various iterations since the demise of chattel slavery. Socially constructed Racism is built, recycled and rebuilt upon the spirit and attitudes of prejudice. There is measurable subconscious, conscious, conceptual, social and legal effects of present day recycled prejudice and power that maintains the status quo of Racism.

Over 400 years the progress has been continually undermined, reconstructed and recycled from chattel slavery, to reconstruction, to sharecropping and convict leasing, to Jim Crow segregation, civil rights, the war on poverty, law and order and the prison industrial complex and present-day culture wars. A multigenerational diminishing and recycling of conditions experienced almost exclusively by African-Americans, Native Americans, and some immigrants in the 400 plus years is required. The hope lies in the generations of x, y and z as the future leadership emerging out of the race-based, social influences on behavior and attitudes of prejudice that support domination of the many by the few, that continues to exist in the land of the free!

The long-term effects of Macro-Aggressions based on the many varieties of prejudice especially racial prejudice are clocked into the nervous system of the Plural body of humanity, reproduced in epigenetic influences on behavior, triggered by subconscious sign stimuli and reinforced by subconscious and conscious Micro-Aggressions. Behavior, attitudes, and social interactions based on subconsciously triggered action patterns that affect all of its victims including the diminishing few who still intent on exercising unrepentant authority, power and privilege. Socially constructed recycled dynamics of prejudice support social hierarchy to preserve power and privilege.

Those of every sort who remain the lowest of the low in the social hierarchy are to be put back in their socially-prescribed, recycled. Socially-constructed influences recycle the good and evil of the artificial culture of race that undermines the shared soul of everyone among the free, in the home of the brave. places according to some reactionaries.

Deliberately-exaggerated socially constructed culture wars are used to reconstruct legal barriers to the teaching of real history and its consequences, prohibiting and silencing free speech, banning books and deconstructing, free thinking, expression and "liberal" or left-wing education. Racism is just one aspect of archetypal, Cultural Insanity that has continually recycled the socially-constructed fear, hate and shame of human hearts and minds by using the socially-constructed language of psychological, social, and emotional denial.

Resistance to changing attitudes is being enshrined in the subtleties of censorship and punishing and outlawing of free speech, gerrymandering and diminishing of voting power, silencing of critics on both sides, loss of jobs by offenders on both sides, the arming of citizens in the name of gun rights and the talk of open rebellion against democracy and the constitution. The present-day, anti-woke agenda is an updated version of the same strategy. Some well-paid celebrities become silent and invisible again, others continue to dribble and entertain, after being well paid and told ever so politely. These are updated examples of the recycling of socially-constructed Macro-Aggressions and Cultural Insanity like the system of sharecropping and the leasing of convict labor based on violations of loitering and vagrancy during Reconstruction. Tactics that provide cheap, unskilled prison labor or provide the nameless numbers to support the $150 billion, yearly profits of the socially-constructed, drug culture as also job security and predatory profits for private prisons. Is the $150 billion profit of the street life drug trade ever deposited in the "Hood" National Bank?

Every sensitive human soul is still "as scared as Hell" by the anomie alienation and incivility engendered by Macro-Aggressions even while scapegoating others of the opposing socially-constructed cultural extremes. As believers in universal justice for every human soul, opponents of socially constructed Macro-Aggressions are deprived of the opportunity of working together by the forces of social conformity that silence dissent. Thus, most tolerate the exaggerated, socially-reconstructed, recycled Micro-Aggressions as that's just the way things work. A socially induced reactionary posture promoted by socially-constructed ego defenses, collective denial, and rationalization produced by Macro-Aggressions. While knowing that "the battle is within" and is won or lost by every human soul too many among the powerful still accept that "such is the way of the world."

The recycling of legally-constructed insanity has continually put racial sentiments in temporary cold storage for future use rather than outlawing its attitudes or eliminating its uncivilized behavior. A socially-constructed strategy of domination by the few over the many as shared human souls continues to deny the promise of justice for all in the land of the free.

Every bird has two wings, or it cannot fly, and most Americans of every sort do not support the socially-constructed extremes of either wing of the socio-political spectrum. So, for the sake of the Almighty, our Great Nation and the future of the Post-Modern World, please do not resuscitate!

Archetypal Culture Wars

The origins of Macro-Aggressions lie in the logic of the original story identifying th Cain Principle of seeking domination over the direction and evolution of the human family as a shared soul that began with the conflicting goals of the archetypal types of the sons of Adam in every soul male and female understood as "Cain - the Industrialist, and Abel - the Socialist." As Imam Mohammed explains:

> *"Instead of the socialist remaining in his own social life and science, the industrialist list became so big that he overcame that movement and brought that movement under material production and under materialism." "Cain was guilty of killing his brother - he killed him while they were at work and spilled his brother's blood on the surface of the earth. That means that he didn't kill a human being outright. That means the materialist socialized the socialist." That is the killing of the shepherd and the killing of his brother. But in the Qur'an, Allah says He was feeling compassion on him because he was feeling sorry about what he had done.*
>
> *And Allah caused a little bird to come where the blood had been spilled on the ground, and the little bird scratched the ground to cover the blood with earth.*
>
> *The brother who was guilty asked, "Why didn't I have the decency to at least cover my brother's blood? That was the beginning of his repenting. It is a very beautiful story." From Life: The Final Battlefield - Part 2 (Note: This part of Imam W. Been Mohammed's Public Address was given after the conclusion of the worldwide radio broadcast.)*

The foundations of democracy are undermined and may even be uprooted entirely when socially-constructed Macro-Aggressions are used to deconstruct the natural spirit of civility. Macro-Aggressions in social policy, customs and law ensure that the shared concerns of privileged citizens are protected while marginalized groups suffer the socially constructed consequence. The need for peace requires real civility, real behavior, attitudes, shared responsibility, and accountability that honor the struggle of real history, for real freedom for every human soul.

The present-day use of the Cain Principle, a possibility in every human soul for seeking to dominate others in fear of losing power, control, profits, and the ability to dominate others. Macro-Aggressions are continually-recycled, in history as barriers that divide the hearts and minds of every citizen in service to protecting some as privileged types among all citizens.

The exaggerated, tall tales of "Critical Race Theory" are a present-day example of dissembling of language and logic in ongoing culture wars as another form of recycled Macro-Aggressions. Race is not a card: race has 400 years of history and socially-constructed insanity drenched in rivers of blood. Critical Race theory is a rationally-constructed use of code words that flip the script of shame, guilt, and blame, as a tactic for falsification, weaponization and denial. This tactic uses coded language to silence social narratives and undermine public perception and employing legal remedies that recycle the insanity that remain in human hearts and minds, while recycling the culture of the privileged few and the Micro-Aggressions that undermine social environments. A Post-modern recycling of 400 years of socially-constructed insanity used deny the real history of lynching, murder, economic exploitation, oppression, segregation, social division and isolation originally created by legalized, violently-enforced, arbitrary racial hatred.

It's Wake-up Time!

The present-day culture wars waged against being "woke" are re-erecting old barriers that aim to contain and recycle the social progress of the last 70 years by reconstructing a new version of a re-segregated ideological confederacy. Blaming critical Race theory and DEI initiatives are culturally-constructed, sleep-inducing strategies that aim to set the freedom struggle back before 1955 when Mother Parks refused to leave her seat so someone more privileged would be comfortable with their privileged feelings. "It's wake-up time" was an original and oft-repeated slogan of the first experience of the original Nation of Islam, and the light of the third resurrection has been on since 1996.

Chapter Fourteen

Rational Influences from Scriptural Reasoning. Establishing Healthy Language Environments, Community Life & Institutional Culture

"We are killing ourselves, going into drugs, wine, prostitution, theft, being recruited by gang leaders, and most of us just sit back and let these things happen.

Sometimes the terrible destiny that God allows to happen is better than the situation that we have for our children at home. That is pitiful. We can become ignorant and become our own oppressors. We can become the very forces that suppress the seeds in our potential and suppress the spirit in that potential. We have to understand the complexity of life and the complexity of society, whether it is in 1986 or earlier. We must understand that there are competing forces and competing systems, and that there are always personal needs.

Many times, these competing forces and systems can become misguided and warped, and an environment will be created that is insane. When that happens, the urge in human potential will begin to emerge, and with the spirit and energy from that human potential will come personalities who will address the wrongs of the environment. They will begin to recommend remedies for correcting the problems of the environment. If we are too caught up in our own traditional ways, too fascinated, charmed and excited over our own achievements, we will not be prepared for the factor of liberation that is emerging in the new individual." — Imam Mohammed, Warith Deen (raa). "Liberty or Death," Muslim Journal, August 28, 1987.

Socially-Constructed Language Barriers To Scriptural Reasoning, Common Sense, & the Universals of Education

Chapter (18) Sūrat l-Kahf (The Cave)

"They said: 'O Zul-qarnain! the Gog and Magog (People) do great mischief on earth: shall we then render thee tribute in order that thou mightest erect a barrier between us and them?'" Al Qur'an, Yusuf Ali, S.18, A.94.

Since the 19th century Industrial Revolution, the content, structure, and goals of public education have been designed to train the masses of common people to serve as skilled and unskilled workers rather than participants in the socially-constructed hierarchy as thinkers and contributors to cultural language and logic. Hierarchy means a "sacred rule" of men, most often established without the direct and necessary support of Scriptural Reasoning or the Guidance of G'd like Rameses II the Pharaoh of Moses and Harun!

Academic, "dry" logic is understood as knowledge that lacks the guidance of moral and ethical clarity for its practical use and application. Present-day academia promotes a high level of sophisticated, intellectually-upgraded, socially and culturally-enslaved service of the spirit and mind to the "dry" logic and amoral utility of reason. An ivory tower, social and politically-constructed hierarchy of scientific dogma and claims of rational and spiritual absolutes that concentrates knowledge and empowers the few in dominating the "anything goes," amoral pursuit of wealth power, and predatory material interests.

One version of the aspirations of predatory interests for the future is for common people to own nothing, be given only what is necessary and be happy. Some among the well-meaning 1% of wealth, power, influence, authoritarian sentiments, and oligarchy plan to own, control and market everything, including the resources of the moon. By G'd's Will, as Creator and Owner of all the Worlds and Systems of Knowledge, no Modern-Day Icarus has wings to land on the sun to extract its light and heat as resources to own and sell!

Al Qur'an, Creation, Rational Sciences & Man's Constructions

Chapter (4) Sūrat l-Nisāa (The Women)

> "O mankind! Verily there hath come to you a convincing proof from your Lord: For We have sent unto you a light (that is) manifest." Al Qur'an, Yusuf Ali, S. 4. A. 173.

As servants of G'd, every believer of every faith tradition with the common sense of life experience, every kind of productive knowledge, ability and social influence is obligated to study from the cradle to the grave. Believers are servants of the common good who share their knowledge to advance the establishment of the common, human soul as a Plural body of humanity and the universals of civilized life. The Prophets (as) are types of the potentials that evolve in the shared soul beginning with Father Adam, male and female.

Our second father is Abraham (as) the Father of Rational Faith for Muslims, Christians and Jews who built the Ka'bah, with his son Ismael (as) and established the ritual language and logic of Hajj, whose rituals represent the spirit for evolving rational faith. As a type in the Plural body of every human soul, the rituals of Abraham represent the establishment of creation-inspired, cultural influences that support the language and logic to help "Remake the World" in accord with rational language and logic and supported by the guidance of revelation and the Will of G'd in creation.

"The Need for Volumes on Science & Scientific Theory"
IWDM

"We really need to write volumes on science or scientific theory. This also includes our perception of the life and nature of the universe itself." — Imam Mohammed, Warith Deen (raa). Ramadan Asr Session, October 29, 2004, Homewood, IL. Lecture.

As a Plural body of believers, goal is for Education for civilized life as defined by the Will of G'd rather than serving only Elites who Master a "little light" that serves only material interest. An artificial darkness without the clear guidance, logic, and support of Scriptural Reasoning. Logic construction currently serves the advancement of Material Sciences alone, supported by elites, elevated by social hierarchies and the academic, "dry" logic of ivory-tower knowledge. As the possessors of power and influence that elevate few in social status, knowledge, power, and privilege Elites who are elevated above the understanding and concerns of the masses.

As common people, descendants, and inheritors of the spirit of enslaved souls, we must begin the construction of academic language and logic at level 4. Idris to build systems of education and the houses of civilized life (called institutions) on the plan of Abraham (as). Academics should support the evolution of Man who is to be responsible for society in the worlds of progress and represented by the Plural body of humanity as Levels 5. Harun, 6. Moses and 7. Abraham of the "world's revolving around a core" of the Ascension of the Soul.

The first three levels of the Ascension of the Soul 1. Adam, 2. Jesus and John and 3. Yusuf are movements in the spiritual nature and sensitivities that are the first and best support for the development of Academics, Science, Reason and Ethics in the common soul. A shura-based approach to education and sharing ideas will allow the common person to participate and compete in contributing to the advancement of the Plural body of society as informed, productive thinkers.

Al Qur'an and the life example of the Prophet (saw) are a definitive guide for application of revelation that informs socially construed logic to benefit all Mankind.

The generations of Muslim African-Americans are uniquely privileged with education in the Social and Material Sciences of the West, the moral and spiritual influences of the Bible, the example of the Prophet (saw), the Qur'an as source and respect for the universal aspirations in America's founding documents and aspirations. values The world of East and West recognizes America's Imam for reawakening the moral excellence that supports rational faith as a renewed approach to civilized progress.

From "Bean Soup Science" to Support of Academics with Scriptural Reasoning

"So, He created Man, firstly, to be responsible in the natural environment, responsible to the Creator in the natural environment. G'd said, 'Whatever is in the sky I made to come down and yield its benefits to you. And whatever is in the earth I made to yield its benefits to you, all people.' So that is the Adam that we have to be reconciled with, if not all of us are going to be cursed down here on this earth. You have to come back and get the mind of the first Man, get the heart of the first Man, male and female. You have to come together in that posture and in that position as the caretaker, custodian and Khalifa — responsible for the environment to your wife, responsible to your children, responsible to your community. You are supposed to be a developer. Allah put Adam in the earth to be a developer, and that is how he became the one qualified to teach even the angels the language, even their own names." — Imam Mohammed, Warith Deen (raa). "Man, and the Universe as Mates Created for Each Other: Its Timeless Relevancy, Session # 5." Ramadan Session. October 15, 2006. Lecture.

The writer's group initiatives established by Imam Warith Deen Mohammed (raa) in the late 1990s spurred the most productive, community effort among common people to write and publish perspectives on Scripture and the Sciences of creation to foster community life and establish institutions. This spirit produced numerous efforts to write and publish materials that continue to benefit the progress of community life among common believers for the Post-Modern World. Establishing academics among descendants of enslaved ancestors who were forbidden to be taught any of the skills or abilities of literacy and learning is a great Mercy and example for the hopes of every human soul.

The writer's group initiative, and the monitoring team that evolved from it, set the example for many other Shura-based organizations as a new approach to the sharing of ideas. The strategy of Imam Mohammed for local leadership and community development proposes that every community in the association establishes Shura-based efforts wherever there are committed believers.

"We Should Come Together, Share What We Have, Then Go Home & Do Our Work."
IWDM

In 2007, Imam Warith Deen Mohammed (raa) urged us to remember that everything in our environment speaks to our minds. Thus, we must be selective about what we allow into our minds because "Words Make People." The Father of Sociology, Ibn Khaldun, explained in his work *Al Muqaddimah* that the act of writing entails the ability to outline and shape letters to indicate what is in one's soul and mind, allowing that person to communicate it to others." Spoken, written — and all other forms of language construction — should reflect one system of knowledge as we follow up on the "Monumental Task" of institutional establishment, the development of language environments, and the principled life of culture and institutions.

While addressing academics and mental health practitioners from across the world, one of our wonderfully insightful sisters working with the community-based initiatives of the Muslim Life Planning Institute (MLPI), pointed out that the progress for our community life is coming from the human soul. The mind and spirit are no longer working separately from the soul. Those who heard this statement from *her* soul can only say that is the Mercy and Guidance of Allah G'd, upon all of His sincere servants.

Shura Baynahum as Sharing of Ideas
Chapter (42) Sūrat l-Shūrā (Consultation)

"Those who hearken to their Lord and establish regular Prayer; who (conduct) their affairs by mutual Consultation; who spend out of what We bestow on them for Sustenance." Al Qur'an, Yusuf Ali, S. 42, A. 38.

Sharing knowledge that establishes a language, logic, and vision of Social and Material Sciences that evolve by a process of Shura, or mutual consultation as a sharing of ideas, is a higher form of democracy for establishing a common vision. Shura is a renewed approach for establishing education and healing for the common soul. The principle of Shura, or "collecting the honey" through collaborative efforts and contributions to institutional memory by resourceful people of every sort benefits the universal Plural body of humanity in every aspect of community life.

The shared blessings of a Plural body of resourceful individuals as committed workers is the most important means for informing the sciences with the keys to Qur'anic language, logic, reason, and wisdom. America's Imam, Imam Warith Deen Mohammed (raa), planted the seeds for a rapidly-blooming, bounteous harvest of healing for the shared soul of the human family. The Imam inspired many among humanity, of every faith, to work together openly to establish a model of universals for advancing education and community life in the land of the free. And we cannot stop now!

A Method of Research from America's Imam
"Test What We are Going to Use."
IWDM

> "I came to the conclusion that if we are to solve our problems we are to (1) first consult the Qur'an and the life of Muhammed the Prophet (saw). After we have gotten the needed material from those two sources, we are created by Allah to (2) make good use of our thoughts, our own ideas, our imagination, skills and resources. We are to test what we are going to use before we use it. We first rely on what has already been revealed in Qur'an and in the life of the Prophet. (3) Test what our minds produce, and, that which is not approved by Qur'an and the Sunnah of the Prophet (saw), reject." — IWDM

Urges as Movements in the Soul
"Four Rivers, Four Birds & Four Mountains in Human Nature as Efforts to Educate & Develop Culture."
IWDM

Chapter (2) Sūrat l-Baqarah (The Cow)

> "When Abraham said: 'Show me, Lord, how You will raise the dead,' He replied: 'Have you no faith?' He said 'Yes, but just to reassure my heart.' Allah said, 'Take four birds, draw them to you, and cut their bodies to pieces. Scatter them over the mountaintops, then call them back. They will come swiftly to you. Know that Allah is Mighty, Wise.'" Al Qur'an, Yusuf Ali, S. 2, A. 260.

One of the basic Qur'anic principles informing this series is the metaphor of Four Mountains that establish life. The four birds cut into pieces and placed on mountains represent movements in the Psyché that begin as two rivers in the soul. The mountains mean "wise, informed, above the small visions." The four birds, inspired by the spirit of thinking and reason, are cut into pieces, and elevated upon four mountains to be climbed. This metaphor represents the establishment of the necessary spirit that inspires reason and wisdom to build all the institutions that support civilized life.

Imam Mohammed (raa) describes mountains as broad vision! Institutions are understood as all the houses of civilized life to be built on a plan for shared vision following the way, or Millah, of Abraham (as) including institutions for establishing and advancing houses of 1. Education, 2. Culture, 3. Business, and 4. Government.

Each of these four domains of universal human need and established life must be tempered and supported by the inspiration of spirit and reason And the birds of inspiration placed on each mountain of wisdom to climb. Each institution must be supported, cross-pollinated, tempered, and moderated by inspiration that supports the integrity of the necessarily-interdependent influences on all four domains of human need. Education is necessary support for the application of culture. Business must be supported by government, and government is a support for Education, Culture and Business.

The mutual consultation of shura is working together to collect honey from "the spacious paths of our Lord" to support every institution so society functions like a busy beehive in the interest of community life. The cross-pollination of influences for every house, as separate but interdependent institutions, represents a sacred trust that requires shared work like that of the bees gathering nectar for the hive. Shared reason, logic and spirit support the vision of each of the institutional domains as universal needs in the shared, human soul and as houses that support universal concerns. The ritual obligations of Hajj provide a complete education for every Muslim, in G'd-given understanding for the spirit and thinking required for building shared vision and supporting the progress of every house and institution.

Social life and the influences of culture and the institutions that establish the four domains should be kept in accord with the natural pattern (Fitratullahi) of the whole creation and the naturally-upright, Fitrah nature of the original soul created Fee Ahsani Taqweem, "in the best of molds." Taqwah is proper regard for the Creator , understood as an urge inherent in every human soul evolving like the movement of rivers from the garden within. The Picto-logic of rivers evolving from the original soul (Adam) created by G'd, is a fundamental principle given as a metaphor required for the evolution of culture. Culture begins with first people or 1. Primal culture that evolves to become 2. traditional cultures and 3. ideological and institutional culture.

The principled logic of Taqwah as proper regard, or G'd-consciousness, for every human soul informs the evolution and proper use of popular culture, entertainment, media, and the oft-misused obligations of politics. Taqwah must be supported by Fujur as the dawning of conscious awareness as Rational Faith.

"Aligning the Natural World & the Social World."

Our strategy for aligning the Social World and the Natural World will make use of Al Qur'an, the life example (Uswah) of the Prophet (saw), Imam Mohammed's Qur'anic commentary on the Ascension of the Soul and other scriptural narratives and universals that inform the Academic Sciences.

This evolving series of topics as monographs draws on specific subject matter informed by the Al Qur'an as Source, Ascension of the Soul, Creation-Inspired Learning that informs Scriptural Reasoning. This paradigm is a framework for addressing the evolution of the soul as: "Culture as Ideas Organized in a Certain Order," "The Natural Urges in

Human Life Give Rise to Social Science," "The Institutions of Social Life and the Logic of Culture," "Isms," "The Development of the Individual and Social Person: Sun – Son – Sound – Senses" and the human person as a Plural body or social or collective self.

"Isms," "How the Mind Can be Deconstructed and Occupied by Abstract Language," "The Principle of Number as the Logic of Abstract Constructions of Language," "The Pen - Philosophical and Social Construction," "Social Passions, Culture and Styles of Life," "Cain - the Industrialist, Abel - the Socialist," "The Body as Language," "Freud and Darwin as 'Isms' in Modern Culture and Social Construction," "The Ancient Temple of Man, Luxor, Egypt, Ancient Mechanisms of Social Conformity and Manipulation of Collective Consciousness" by Imam Warith Deen Mohammed

A Model for Evolving Freedom, Free Thinking, Collaborative Effort, Shared Vision, Local Responsibility & Leadership
"African-American Leadership."
IWDM

> *"Dear beloved people, we have to have a grip on our life. We have to have leaders that are not made by outsiders. You have never been successful with a leader that was made by an outsider. Praise be to Allah; you have a leader in me that is not made by an outsider. I have depended solely on my own ability to go on the urge of truth, honesty, sincerity, well-meaning, good person, and to trust Allah, that Allah will guide me, Allah will help me."* — Imam Mohammed, Warith Deen (raa). "Imam Mohammed Speaks from Harlem, N.Y." Symbolic Language. 1984, Harlem, NY. Lecture.

As educator Dr. Jon Yasin points out, our task as education workers is monumental, and we thank Allah (swt) for the consistent progress of our now 20 + years of shared effort on this collective —

third shift of the generations with origins in the original Nation of Islam, as servants of His cause, and many of us are working double and triple shifts! Al Humdullilah! Application of the principled logic and strategic implications of the Ascension of the Soul, Imam Mohammed's directives, the organizational principles for making knowledge whole are keys to progress. Qur'anic sources of language and logic, the Ascension of the soul and Creation-Inspired learning are a wholistic context for reeducating ourselves about all aspects of how we search, research, teach and learn that serves us more completely in our "Sacred Matter" of education than other modern-day foundations of education, East or West! The path forward will require long-term collective commitment, leadership as service and inter-generational effort. With G'd-given Mercy, the spirit and work established by the generations before us, the Holy Book (Al Qur'an) and the Prophet's life example (saw) guiding our spirit and with a mind to achieve G'd-given understanding, we will excel in every way to achieve our monumental task, In Shaa Allah!

"We can work together, cooperate with each other for the same goals and benefit from each other's resources, vision, knowledge, in Islam and in our professions. So, that is what we would like. That would be the best way to get it." — Imam Mohammed, Warith Deen (raa). "Muhammad Speaks." Muslim Journal. January 1, 1982 – January 8, 1982. Interview.

And we Pray that Allah (swt) — Al Aziz, Al Hakim, Rabil Alamin — continues to Bless our efforts of working together as common humanity for establishment of the universal soul."

HAE © June 27th, 2023, Yaum Arafah, 9 Dhul Hijjah, 1444 AH

Epilogue & Past as Prologue

Evolving a Series of Studies
Chapter (2) Sūrat l-Baqarah (The Cow)

> "Behold, thy Lord said to the angels: 'I will create a vicegerent on earth.' They said: 'Wilt Thou place therein one who will make mischief therein and shed blood? - whilst we do celebrate Thy praises and glorify Thy holy (name)?' He said: 'I know what ye know not.'" Al Qur'an, Yusuf Ali, S. 2. A. 30.

The purpose of an epilogue as a conclusion for the present work must look to the past in anticipation of the future. This epilogue as an evolving narrative of past and prologue also looks to the future in anticipation of Mankind evolving as a Plural body from Father Adam (as) as the custodian of creation Allah speaks of in Al Qur'an, S. 2, A. 30. In the context of the evolution of creation, Adam the common soul is the Plural body of all Mankind that evolves as spirit and thinking, created from a single soul, male and female, (Nafsin Wahidah). Adam, male and female, is created as mind for as the caretaker of creation the destiny intended by G'd for humanity.

The particulars of this epilogue speak in part to the goal of presenting a series of monographs that address the long-standing, rapidly-passing, 400-year-old, constantly-recycled struggle of the strange, once-upon-a-time philosophy of both former "colored folk" and "masters." The Plural body of a nation whose spirit has been colored with rational exaggerations made of skin. The shared future must be understood as a destiny for shared souls who are free of the continual recycling of social-constructions that market skin, gender identity and other deconstructed language, logic, and corrupt influences of culture. Influences that promote different brands of men as mind and inferior or superior brands of the human soul. A strategy of dividing to conquer the soul by promoting socially-constructed denials and language barriers to shared humanity that devolve into dog-eat-dog" social and cultural conflicts!

A socially-constructed, exaggerated conflict of skin, gender, ethnic, tribal, or religion as artificial socially constructed divisions misused in dominating of shared perception and constructing culture for ruling humanity as Adam (as) as mind and spirit. As the most exploited souls and socially-constructed "lowest of the low," a mercy for African-Americans was being left out of the benefits from the rationally-constructed scheme. Alhumdulillah! A strategy for the self-interested domination, and rule, of the Man-Made world for material benefit.

Eliminating the socially constructed degradation of the common soul is a Post-Modern imperative for seeking the guidance of faith and the great mercy of repentance as a necessity for redemption of the shared soul. As an answer to 400 years of the unceasing prayers of humanity, this hope is a certain blessing evolving in our present-day, social circumstances.

Natural Urges in Human Life, Give Rise to Social Science, the Logic & Ethics of Institutions, Culture & Civilized Life!

"We live in cities now and buildings are all around. Man's creations have shut out G'd's creations." — Imam Mohammed, Warith Deen (raa). Curriculum Meeting, 2001, Harvey, IL. Lecture.

As a continuing series of monographs, this effort is in service to a major principle of traditional academic discourse cited by Imam Warith Deen Mohammed (raa), "Competing with those who have higher knowledge." The topics to be covered in this evolving series of proposed monographs will also reflect principled logic that represents an emerging Post-Modern view. A wholistic view of principled logic that will help clarify history, the Academic Sciences, research methods and processes for evolving civilized life based on the emerging principles of Scriptural Reasoning.

The Ascension-of-the-Soul-based premise redefines academics as a potential in every human soul. This effort aims to support the original sense and proper use of academics in evolving science as "The Lost Property of the Believer." One of the specific goals is evolving Scriptural Reasoning for establishing, advancing, and preserving shared vision, memory language and logic for "an institution that will outlive us all" as charged by Imam Mohammed (raa). A mandate given directly by Imam Mohammed (raa)for the education work of the Sister Clara Mohammed Foundation and Clearing House. This idea also represents a nontraditional purpose for academic discourse. That is:

> 'Educated professionals are to translate language to benefit the common Man's productivity.'" — Imam Mohammed, Warith Deen (raa). "Ramadan Session." 2005, Lecture.

This vision represents a forward-looking approach to Shura Baynahum, or mutual consultation as a sharing of ideas, as a new approach to establishing and evolving academics, servant leadership and principles of democracy.

> "We should come together, share what we have, then go home and do our work." — Imam Mohammed, Warith Deen (raa), August 3, 2008, Homewood, IL. 1st Sunday Lecture.

A specific goal of proposing this collaborative model is to establish the work of the Sister Clara Muhammad Memorial Education

Foundation Clearing House and workgroup as a model for promoting shared vision, free thinking, local leadership, shared hands-on work, individual responsibility and local authority toward the establishment of an institution that will "outlive us all" (Imam W.D. Mohammed).

"Knowledge Frees Everyone." — IWDM

**We Live by Faith,
We Progress by Knowledge & Reason.**

Chapter (96) Sūrat l-'Alaq (The Clot)

"Nay, but man doth transgress all bounds."
"In that he looketh upon himself as self-sufficient."
Al Qur'an, Yusuf Ali. S. 96, A. 6-7.

A Personal Reflection from a Letter to a Childhood Friend

This epilogue, and past as prologue, originally began as a personal reflection addressed to a life-long, faithful, Christian friend. In that spirit, this series of monographs is intended to promote universal understanding for the common soul, the success of which rests entirely in the hands of the Almighty! Every human person draws on faith, common sense and the shared knowledge and wisdom of family, committed friends, formal education, fellow workers, and many other citizens as a Plural body for the many, concrete, and abstract lessons that support and evolve civilized life! Such work in service to the universal peace of social sentiments is an obligation to the common soul, the community of humanity and the worldview for Post-Modern universals that is becoming increasingly necessary for the rapidly changing and — some suppose rapidly-concluding — Man-Made world.

There are many who submit to the proposition that the Man-Made world is concluding, but we may suppose that only as the world of

Man has been structured abstractly, ideologically, and culturally by those aiming to continue the predatory, self-interested domination of the soul of the past 500 years of history called "Modernism." Even now in the Post-Modern World, competition for dominion and rule over the material world and all human souls is based on the flawed idea, and Darwinian supposition, of merit as the amoral survival of the fittest and other logically-deconstructed, exaggerated notions of the primal motives of men. Some of those among the souls of Man as mind, male and female, are still seen by other men as no more than animal life. I would never have anticipated the dream life journey that continues into eight decades, the privileges of a small-town, segregated, Southern upbringing where only a very few ever failed. A handful, even among the "underprivileged," many of whom excelled in unimaginable, and profound ways. A mercy complemented by grounding in the compromise of Booker T. Washington, my grandparents' bootstrap Tuskegee roots and the bountiful harvest from Dr G. W. Carver's garden, from which many sciences bloomed. The upliftment of the many by the small-town, dedicated heroes of a segregated-but-privileged youth of a "renaissance" city named Florence, with an entire community of caring parents, teachers and peers from the very poorest of circumstances. Yes, bootleggers and men who shined shoes included, whose descendants have excelled far beyond all plans, aspirations, seeming possibilities and expectations.

And the hard-won honor of being a leader of combat infantry soldiers in one of Mankind's many, senseless wars. A war preceded and followed directly by the great fortune of a college education, working, living, and learning in the revolutionary 1970's at an upper crust, "old money," Seven Sisters institution (yes, Sisters). The marvel of graduate education from a university affectionately nicknamed a "zoo" by its graduates and admirers and the sacred obligations of being a college teacher.

Like the generation of many baby boomers, I share the urge for freedom, directly from the genes of both slaves and slave masters. An urge for every soul made a slave to socially-constructed, cultural influences, that continue to enslave and segregate, and an urge encompassing everything in the scope of 400 years of genetic memory striving for the freedom born in the U.S.A.

What a marvel we are as a generation of baby boomers who have not completed our work toward the shared legacy we must leave for generations X, Y and Z or perish together as fools! We have not been relieved of the duty to do so personally, clocked into our genes as a debt in a "day of debt" and a demand on our shared souls.

As the post-WWII generation in the multi-cultural melting pot of America, we were not motivated by "the greatest generation" of our parents so that our yearnings and our destiny were only for personal achievement, status, material wealth and power. In that sense, we are the last and most influential generation still connected with our inherited social sentiments and hard-earned wisdom intact to pass on to future generations.

None of us knows the "apocalyptic" absolutes or the final destiny for Man and the Man-Made world, no matter the pretense of the many, modern, would-be "Pharaohs," of whose motives and schemes we may have only a hint. We submit to the premise that our nation and planet are not in danger of crumbling apocalyptically. Now approaching 80 years old, I encourage the faithful of the whole generation of fellow Baby Boomers of every color, belief and persuasion to think, feel and continue to work as if we will never grow old, until we all fade away like all old soldiers! None of us knows the "apocalyptic" absolutes or the final destiny for Man and the Man-Made world, no matter the pretense of the many, modern, would-be "pharaohs," of whose motives and schemes we have only a hint. We submit to the premise that our planet is not in danger of crumbling apocalyptically and the natural sensitivities and potential of our shared humanity are not disappearing even if the man-made hell grows hotter.

As the first generation of American teenagers, Baby Boomers also understand the "I got this" impulsivity of the recently "woke" generation of our children, grandchildren and now our great-grandchildren — with whom we struggle to keep from being lulled to sleep in the socially-constructed, Cultural Insanity of a woke and anti-woke world. Those who still have shared, social sensitivities intact can already clearly see the aim of that exaggerated deconstruction of the culture wars fostering recycled division and the politically-and-archetypally-constructed denial of almost 70 years of hard-earned lessons for our nation and world. A repeat of the recycled regression at the end of the era of Reconstruction in 1867.

The Civil War fostered the era of Jim Crow lynchings and other irrational exaggerations, denials, Micro-Aggressions, Cultural Insanity, prohibitions, and barriers to the actual facts of history and a final cure for the exaggerations, falsifications and pretenses about the nature of the shared human soul. Most of the citizenry of our nation remain wide awake even in old age, and no socially-constructed lullabies of politically-motivated Pied Pipers or schemers will make us nod out.

Those who oppose the evolution of Adam, the universal human soul, knowingly deconstruct, reinvent, and recycle the socially-constructed influences that corrupt the shared, social sentiments. By G'd's Will, we pray we never lose the vision of freedom, justice, and equality that we learned by heart at our 60's breakfast tables.

Like many others, this work is a duty upon our individual souls and anything that results of benefit beyond that is not for us as the final judge. And the inevitable flaws of every human person are, however, certainly my own. Every person needs a witness that won't dial 911 for the men with the white coats to dress you in long, white sleeves that cross your arms in the front then tie behind your back to cuff your hands. Until now , there were perhaps less than a handful of people I could ever say such things to without my sanity being called into question, and many among my very best, life-long, faithful friends are already in the life hereafter.

Thank the Almighty, Most Gracious, Most Merciful for His Guidance and Mercy, the example of the seal of the Prophets, Muhammad of Arabia (saw) the guidance and mercy for Mankind. And all the Prophets, known and unknown, of every nation, tribe, and people for establishing Freedom, Justice, and Equality for the shared, human soul, with sincerity of faith and heartfelt confidence in the G'd-given destiny for all Mankind.

1 Dhul Qidah, 1444 AH, (5/21/2023)

Poem

Mr. Jefferson of Monticello

The divided soul rejoins, in its proper form,
Built upon the blue-green sanctuary, an original designed with no back door.

Evoking the universal goodness, of being an American,
From a generational exile of downtrodden Africa,
Who enters, thankfully upon its enriched cultivation.
Out of the inequality of Sally's belly, that is our mutual hell…

The design for a timeless liberty, from a brief stay of youth, in wooded forests and blue hills. Built of brick and oak, finished with pine, furnished with cedar.

Liberty that enters the shelter, from East and West,
Clarified by sky light, telescope, microscope, philosophic, scientific, sacred texts, and old Europa's finest glass….

Preserving the sustenance of 200 years ….
For every schoolchild……at four cents an acre.
Stored upon her overflowing shelves….
The hard-earned harvest of the honeybee,
A smugglers pocketful, of meager rice
And every fertile idea parceled out,

For any curious mind to find…and replant
A ransom for the freedom of slave and master,

And beginning an ever-New World
From here to a still distant, far western sea……

Curiosity and secular manhood
Shaped from the pages of Creation,
Some foolishly say, true faith abandoned,
Ticking trustfully… by natures archaic clock
Counting the return to a day of restoral
From the thankless sea of a grateful Jonah.

Perfecting still virgin hopes….
Bussed, going, and coming…...On newly paved paths,
In ruts of old wagons, upon once wearied horses,
Well-worn trail, of owned….and hired hand.
Joining in faith with the rightful owner's eternal design
For a true freedom ride…. up….and down…...
The fertile valley………. of our unfinished soul………

Charlottesville, V.A. © 7/23/08

About the Author

The Writer/Scribe of this series, Hameed El Amin is a retired college and university level Psychology and Social Science teacher who facilitates work for the development of education for schools. Dr El Amin has clinical, counseling, teaching, and consulting experience with varied populations from children to adults in Massachusetts, New Jersey, Alabama, and Michigan. Dr El Amin earned a BA from Morehouse College, a Master of Science degree in Biological Psychology and a Ph.D. in Clinical and Social Ecology from the University of Massachusetts, Amherst.

Dr. El Amin has worked with the Mosque Cares Education team under the leadership of Imam Warith Deen Mohammed (raa) and currently works with the Sister Clara Muhammad Memorial Education Foundation and Clara Muhammad Schools Consortium established by Imam Mohammed prior to his passing. Dr El Amin works with organizations supporting education for developing community schools from California to Bermuda as well as local, national, and international education and interfaith efforts. Dr El Amin is also a veteran of the Vietnam War where he served as a Combat Infantry Officer.

Writer/Scribe

Chapter (96) Sūrat l-'Alaq (The Clot)

1."Proclaim! (or read!) in the name of thy Lord and Cherisher, Who created - 2. Created Man, out of a (mere) clot of congealed blood: 3. Proclaim! And thy Lord is Most Bountiful, - 4. He Who taught (the use of) the pen, - 5. Taught Man that which he knew not." Al Qur'an, Yusuf Ali, S. 96. A. 1–5.

The term Writer/Scribe more accurately describes the proper role in shura-based, group efforts for attribution as a title. All of those who take the shared responsibility for articulating and recording the shared ideas, knowledge and wisdom share in the benefit of the healing that comes with "collecting the honey" through a shura-based sharing of ideas. So, free your soul and your mind to free the people!

Abbreviations

(SAW) or (AS) – Salla-llahu Alayhi Wa Sallam, Peace Be Upon Him (or them) – a salutation to the Prophet Muhammad (saw) and all the Prophets (as)

(RAA) – Rahima Allahu Alai – G'd's Mercy Be Upon Him (a prayer for the dead)

IWDM – Imam Warith Deen Mohammed

THEM – The Honorable Elijah Muhammad

S. – Surah – A chapter of the Holy Qur'an

A. – Ayah, Verse – A verse of the Holy Qur'an

SWT – Subhana Wa Ta-'ala – Highly Praised Is He (G'd, Allah)

ISA – In Sha Allah – If G'd Wills

Collaboration:

The Education Workgroup of the Sister Clara Mohammed Education Consortium, Sister Clara Muhammed Memorial Education Foundation & Clearing House.

Works Cited & References

Bible Gateway, www.biblegateway.com.

Harper, Douglas. Lui, Chongwei, "Etymology of architect." Online Etymology Dictionary, https://www.etymonline.com/word/architect. Accessed 31 January, 2024.

Harper, Douglas. Lui, Chongwei, "Etymology of axiom." Online Etymology Dictionary, https://www.etymonline.com/word/axiom. Accessed 31 January, 2024.

Harper, Douglas. Lui, Chongwei, "Etymology of deconstruction." Online Etymology Dictionary, https://www.etymonline.com/word/deconstruction. Accessed 31 January, 2024.

Harper, Douglas. Lui, Chongwei, "Etymology of devolution." Online Etymology Dictionary, https://www.etymonline.com/word/devolution. Accessed 31 January, 2024.

Harper, Douglas. Lui, Chongwei, "Etymology of dissemble." Online Etymology Dictionary, https://www.etymonline.com/word/dissemble. Accessed 31 January, 2024.

Harper, Douglas. Lui, Chongwei, "Etymology of dogma." Online Etymology Dictionary, https://www.etymonline.com/word/dogma. Accessed 31 January, 2024.

Harper, Douglas. Lui, Chongwei, "Etymology of elite." Online Etymology Dictionary, https://www.etymonline.com/word/elite. Accessed 31 January, 2024.

Harper, Douglas. Lui, Chongwei, "Etymology of engineer." Online Etymology Dictionary, https://www.etymonline.com/word/engineer. Accessed 31 January, 2024.

Harper, Douglas. Lui, Chongwei, "Etymology of epistemology." Online Etymology Dictionary, https://www.etymonline.com/word/epistemology. Accessed 31 January, 2024.

Harper, Douglas. Lui, Chongwei, "Etymology of etymology." Online Etymology Dictionary, https://www.etymonline.com/word/etymology. Accessed 31 January, 2024.

Harper, Douglas. "Lui, Chongwei, Etymology of evolution." Online Etymology Dictionary, https://www.etymonline.com/word/evolution. Accessed 31 January, 2024.

Harper, Douglas. Lui, Chongwei, "Etymology of genesis." Online Etymology Dictionary, https://www.etymonline.com/word/genesis. Accessed 31 January, 2024.

Harper, Douglas. Lui, Chongwei, "Etymology of genius." Online Etymology Dictionary, https://www.etymonline.com/word/genius. Accessed 31 January 2024.

Harper, Douglas. Lui, Chongwei, "Etymology of logos." Online Etymology Dictionary, https://www.etymonline.com/word/Logos. Accessed 31 January, 2024.

Harper, Douglas. Lui, Chongwei, "Etymology of media." Online Etymology Dictionary, https://www.etymonline.com/word/media. Accessed 31 January, 2024.

Harper, Douglas. Lui, Chongwei, "Etymology of metaphysic." Online Etymology Dictionary, https://www.etymonline.com/word/metaphysic. Accessed 31 January, 2024.

Harper, Douglas. Lui, Chongwei, "Etymology of mind." Online Etymology Dictionary, https://www.etymonline.com/word/mind. Accessed 31 January, 2024.

Harper, Douglas. Lui, Chongwei, "Etymology of principle." Online Etymology Dictionary, https://www.etymonline.com/word/principle. Accessed 31 January 2024.

Harper, Douglas. Lui, Chongwei, "Etymology of School." Online Etymology Dictionary, https://www.etymonline.com/word/social. Accessed 31 January, 2024.

Harper, Douglas. Lui, Chongwei, "Etymology of progress." Online Etymology Dictionary, https://www.etymonline.com/word/progress. Accessed 31 January, 2024.

Harper, Douglas. Lui, Chongwei, "Etymology of science." Online Etymology Dictionary, https://www.etymonline.com/word/science. Accessed 31 January, 2024.

Harper, Douglas. Lui, Chongwei, "Etymology of social." Online Etymology Dictionary, https://www.etymonline.com/word/social. Accessed 31 January, 2024.

Harper, Douglas. Lui, Chongwei, "Etymology of sole." Online Etymology Dictionary, https://www.etymonline.com/word/sole. Accessed 31 January, 2024.

Harper, Douglas. Lui, Chongwei, "Etymology of soul." Online Etymology Dictionary, https://www.etymonline.com/word/soul. Accessed 31 January, 2024.

Harper, Douglas. Lui, Chongwei, "Etymology of study." Online Etymology Dictionary, https://www.etymonline.com/word/study. Accessed 31 January, 2024.

Harper, Douglas. Lui, Chongwei, "Etymology of think." Online Etymology Dictionary, https://www.etymonline.com/word/think. Accessed 31 January, 2024.

References

Heisenberg, Werner. Lui, Chongwei, "Quantum-Theoretical Reinterpretation of Kinematic and Mechanical Relations." Translated by Tomáš Mančal. Zeitschrift fur Physik, 33, 1925, 879-893. www.arxiv.org/abs/2108.03119.

Mohammed, Imam Warith Deen. "A Community for All People." New Africa Radio, Progressions Magazine, Oct. 1985, newafricaradio.com/articles/november-85-1.html. Accessed 25 Jan. 2024.

Mohammed, Imam Warith Deen (raa). "Adult Dawah." March 20, 2005, Chicago, IL. Lecture.

Mohammed, Imam Warith Deen (raa). August 3, 2008. Homewood, IL. Lecture.

Mohammed, Imam Warith Deen (raa). "By the Token of Time, By the Hour." April 12, 2002, Salatul Jumu'ah Khutbah at the Atlanta Masjid of Al-Islam. Atlanta, GA.

Mohammed, Imam Warith Deen (raa). "Circumcision of the Mind." Imams Meeting, 1997, Masjid Bilal, Cleveland, OH. Lecture.

Mohammed, Imam Warith Deen (raa). "Curriculum Meeting," 2001, Harvey, IL. Lecture.

Mohammed, Imam Warith Deen (raa). "Educational Concerns." Historic Sedalia Address, 9 April 1982. Lecture.

Mohammed, Imam Warith Deen (raa). "Genetic Memory, Community as the Focus for Life - Part II." Lecture

Mohammed, Imam Warith Deen (raa). "Gog and Magog," Muslim Journal, October 31, 1986.

Mohammed, Imam Warith Deen (raa). "Imams Retreat Part II." 16 January 16, 1999, Randolph, VA. Lecture.

Mohammed, Imam Warith Deen (raa). "Imams Retreat III." January 16, 1999, Randolph, VA. Lecture.

Mohammed, Imam Warith Deen (raa). "Liberating the Community (Allah Takes Care of the Future)." June 17, 2007. Raleigh, NC. Lecture.

Mohammed, Imam Warith Deen (raa). "Liberty or Death," Muslim Journal, August 28, 1987.

Mohammed, Imam Warith Deen (raa). "Looking For Happiness, Conceptual Wholeness (Four Sacred Conflicts)." Ramadan Session, 2002, Chicago, IL. Lecture.

Mohammed, Imam Warith Deen (raa). "Man, and the Universe as Mates Created for Each Other: Its Timeless Relevancy, Session # 5." Ramadan Session. October 15, 2006. Lecture.

Mohammed, Imam Warith Deen (raa). May 26, 1991, Nashville, TN. Lecture.

Mohammed, Imam Warith Deen (raa). "Moses by Name in the Qur'an More Than Any Other Prophet." Imams Meeting. February 12, 1983. Dallas, TX. Lecture.

Mohammed, Imam Warith Deen (raa). "Muhammad Speaks." Muslim Journal. January 1, 1982 – January 8, 1982. Interview.

Mohammed, Imam Warith Deen (raa). "Natural Evolution Blocked by Man's Constructions." May 26, 1991. Nashville, TN. Lecture.

Mohammed, Imam Warith Deen (raa). "Ramadan Sessions, Asr Session." 29 October 2004. Homewood, IL. Lecture.

Mohammed, Imam Warith Deen (raa). "Ramadan Session." 2005. Lecture.

Mohammed, Imam Warith Deen (raa). "Ramadan Session." 2006. Lecture.

Mohammed, Imam Warith Deen (raa). "Savior Day," Muslim Journal. February 26, 2002. Charleston, S.C.

Mohammed, Imam Warith Deen (raa). "Symbolic Language." 1984, Harlem, N.Y. Lecture.

Mohammed, Imam Warith Deen (raa). "Symbolic Language." Imam W. Deen Muhammed speaks from Harlem, N.Y. 1984, Harlem, NY. Lecture.

Kariger & Fierro. Etymology of ius." Online Dictionary,

https: //www.dictionary.com. Accessed 1 February 2024.

King James Bible Online, www.kingjamesbibleonline.org/.

Koon, Jeffrey Winter. *Cultural Insanity, the Key to Understanding Our World & Ourselves: With Current Political and Environmental Examples, and Historical Case Studies in Witch Hunting, the Medieval Church Impeding Science, and the Rejection of Geologic Time & Evolution (the Original and Definitive Account)*. BookBaby, 2021.

Linné, Carl Von. Carolus Linnaeus Systema Naturae, "System of Nature Through the Three Kingdoms of Nature." 1735.

Pierce, Chester M. Alen, Gail B. *Childism,* Psychiatric Annals , V 5, No. 7, July 1st, 1975

Shuaibe, Imam Faheem, "The Reality of Our Sacred Nature: Our Origins and Our Destiny," Unpublished manuscript.

Tattersall, Ian. "Homo sapiens." Encyclopedia Britannica, 3 Jan. 2024, https://www.britannica.com/topic/Homo-sapiens.

The Noble Quran, www.quran.com.

The Quranic Arabic Corpus, www.corpus.quran.com

"The Slave Girl Shall Give Birth to Her Master." Hadith, A Saying of the Prophet (saw), Sahih Muslim 9. www.sunnah.com/muslim:9.

Citations of Sura & Ayat of Al Qur'an

Al Qur'an, Yusuf Ali, S. 90, A. 8-10. www.corpus.quran.com
Al Qur'an, Yusuf Ali, S. 90, A. 12-13. www.corpus.quran.com
Al Qur'an, Yusuf Ali, S. 28, A. 77. www.corpus.quran.com
Al Qur'an, Yusuf Ali, S. 41, A. 53. www.corpus.quran.com
Al Qur'an, Yusuf Ali, S. 31, A. 27. www.corpus.quran.com
Al Qur'an, Yusuf Ali, S. 16, A. 48. www.corpus.quran.com
Al Qur'an, Yusuf Ali, S. 2, A. 33. www.corpus.quran.com
Al Qur'an, Yusuf Ali, S. 36, A. 37. www.corpus.quran.com
Al Qur'an, Yusuf Ali, S. 2, A. 37. www.corpus.quran.com
Al Qur'an, Yusuf Ali. S.6, A. 98. www.corpus.quran.com
Al Qur'an, Yusuf Ali, S. 2, A. 117. www.corpus.quran.com
Al Qur'an, Yusuf Ali, S. 51, A. 56. www.corpus.quran.com
Al Qur'an, Yusuf Ali, S.6, A.19. www.corpus.quran.com
Al Qur'an, Yusuf Ali, S. 21, A. 104. www.corpus.quran.com
Al Qur'an, Yusuf Ali, S.6, A. 59. www.corpus.quran.com
Al Qur'an, Yusuf Ali, S. 17, A. 85. www.corpus.quran.com
Al Qur'an, Yusuf Ali, S. 91, A. 7-8. www.corpus.quran.com
Al Qur'an, Yusuf Ali, S. 2, A. 187. www.corpus.quran.com
Al Qur'an, Yusuf Ali, S. 29, A. 49. www.corpus.quran.com
Al Qur'an, Yusuf Ali, S. 95, A. 4-5. www.corpus.quran.com
Al Qur'an, Yusuf Ali, S. 49, A. 13. www.corpus.quran.com
Al Qur'an, Yusuf Ali, S. 15, A 28-29. www.corpus.quran.com
Al Qur'an, Yusuf Ali, S. 15, A 28-29. www.corpus.quran.com
Al Qur'an, Yusuf Ali, S. 78. A. 19. www.corpus.quran.com
Al Qur'an, Yusuf Ali, S. 96. A. 1-5. www.corpus.quran.com
Al Qur'an, Yusuf Ali, S. 30, A. 21. www.corpus.quran.com
Al Qur'an, Yusuf Ali, S. 34, A.12 – 13. www.corpus.quran.com
Al Qur'an, Yusuf Ali, S. 65, A. 12. www.corpus.quran.com

Al Qur'an, Yusuf Ali, S. 96. A. 1-5. www.corpus.quran.com
Al Qur'an, Yusuf Ali, S. 24, A. 35. www.corpus.quran.com
Al Qur'an, Yusuf Ali, S. 2, A.102. www.corpus.quran.com
Al Qur'an, Yusuf Ali, S. 41, A. 53. www.corpus.quran.com
Al Qur'an, Yusuf Ali, S. 17. A. 85. www.corpus.quran.com
Al Qur'an, Yusuf Ali, S. 20. A. 50. www.corpus.quran.com
Al Qur'an, Yusuf Ali, S. 16, A. 89. www.corpus.quran.com
Al Qur'an, Yusuf Ali, S. 16, A. 48. www.corpus.quran.com
Al Qur'an, Yusuf Ali, S. 95, A. 1-3. www.corpus.quran.com
Al Qur'an, Yusuf Ali, S. 29, A. 41. www.corpus.quran.com
Al Qur'an, Yusuf Ali, S. 87, A. 1-3. www.corpus.quran.com
Al Qur'an, Yusuf Ali, S. 20, A. 50. www.corpus.quran.com
Al Qur'an, Yusuf Ali, S. 36, A. 37. www.corpus.quran.com
Al Qur'an, Yusuf Ali, S. 14, A. 24. www.corpus.quran.com
Al Qur'an, Yusuf Ali, S. 14, A. 24. www.corpus.quran.com
Al Qur'an, Yusuf Ali, S. 7, A. 16. www.corpus.quran.com
Al Qur'an, Yusuf Ali, S. 3, A. 59. www.corpus.quran.com
Al Qur'an, Yusuf Ali, S. 2, A. 127. www.corpus.quran.com
Al Qur'an, Yusuf Ali, S.32, A.5. www.corpus.quran.com
Al Qur'an, Yusuf Ali, S. 95, A. 41-3. www.corpus.quran.com
Al Qur'an, Yusuf Ali, S. 38 A. 75-76. www.corpus.quran.com
Al Qur'an, Yusuf Ali, S.2, A. 34. www.corpus.quran.com
Al Qur'an, Sahih International S. 21, A. 107.www.corpus.quran.com

Al Qur'an, 7, Yusuf Ali, Ayat 12 " I am better from Him."
(Ana Kairun Minhu.) www.corpus.quran.com
Al Qur'an, S.18, A.94. www.corpus.quran.com
Al Qur'an, Yusuf Ali, S. 4. A. 173. www.corpus.quran.com
Al Qur'an, Yusuf Ali, S. 42, A. 38. www.corpus.quran.com
Al Qur'an, Yusuf Ali, S. 2, A. 260. www.corpus.quran.com
Al Qur'an, Yusuf Ali, S. 2. A.30. www.corpus.quran.com
Al Qur'an, Yusuf Ali, S. 96. A. 1-5. www.corpus.quran.com

> ### "I Got Shoes"
> ### Old Negro Spiritual
>
> "I got shoes, you got shoes,
> When we get to Heaven, gonna put on our shoes!"

New Shoes Educational Publishers

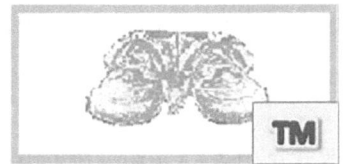

About the Cover

I took this photo of the River Buna & Tekki House at Blagaj in Bosnia-Herzegovina during one of my travels. It depicts for me, in an abstract way, man's relationship with the earth, the rivers, the heavens, and Allah's creation as a whole.

The River Buna Flows from a Karstic Spring Hidden beneath the Dinaric Alps, at the town of Blagaj near Mostar, Bosnia-Herzegovina

www.ingramcontent.com/pod-product-compliance
Lightning Source LLC
Chambersburg PA
CBHW030518080526
44586CB00011B/244